Mary Burritt Christiansen Poetry Series

Vincent Barrett Price,
SERIES EDITOR

OTHER TITLES AVAILABLE IN THE
University of New Mexico Press
Mary Burritt Christiansen Poetry Series:

Miracles of Sainted Earth
Victoria Edwards Tester

Poets of the Non-Existent City
Estelle Gershgoren Novak

Selected Poems of Gabriela Mistral
Translated and edited by Ursula K. Le Guin

Deeply Dug In
R. L. Barth

Amulet Songs: Poems Selected and New
Lucile Adler

In Company: An Anthology of New Mexico Poets
edited by Lee Bartlett, V. B. Price,
and Dianne Edenfield Edwards

Tiempos Lejanos
Nasario García

Refuge of Whirling Light

Frontispiece and back page:
Details from pastel painting by the author.

refuge
of
whirling
light

poems

ⓖ ⓖ ⓖ

MARY BEATH

UNIVERSITY OF NEW MEXICO PRESS

ALBUQUERQUE

ⓑ ⓑ ⓑ

Library of Congress Cataloging-in-Publication Data

Beath, Mary, 1950—
Refuge of whirling light : poems / Mary Beath.
p. cm.   (Mary Burritt Christiansen poetry series)
ISBN 0-8263-3422-9 (Cloth : alk. paper)
I. Title. II. Series.
PS3602.E263R44 2005
811'.6–dc22
2004020777

ⓑ ⓑ ⓑ

Design and composition: Mina Yamashita

for Kit

Contents

foreword

When I first started reading Mary Beath's poems more than a decade ago, I was immediately impressed by how she traversed the terrains of multiple genres and candidly faced the uncensored realities of what it means to be alive in the universe of flesh and bones, neither abandoning nor becoming lost in the universe of science and ideas. Some of her poems are almost novelesque, t e lling absorbing stories with descriptive eloquence. All her works are devoted to understanding what experience means. She has the attention to detail of someone trained both in b i o logy and in the arts. Her interests are intrepidly eclectic. It doesn't take her readers long to realize, either, that she's writing from her direct experience as a woman who is self-reliant enough to hike and camp alone in the wilderness of the west, who is independent enough to live the kind of life that suits her, and is matter-of-fact enough to write as she likes across a wide horizon of reality from living ecologies to ecologies of love to how a mind and body become a single place, uni que as any landscape.

Her poems belong, in part, to an engendered world of American letters that deals with thriving in a time of intense and dangerous transition, a time in which a world society based on exploi tation is slowly crumbling, a time in which knowing one's place in the landscape is as important as knowing how one's personality and struggle for authenticity have evolved.

As a poet she holds that "we needn't compartmentalize our experiences, sequestering nature from human sensuality, from emotion, from language, from ideas."

In her poem "Go West," Beath writes

I set out west one June morning at dawn,
sun at my back, full moon
straight ahead. Nothing more profound
than possibility. . . .
Yet lack of intent matters little to the
heart's response: to open. To open like
the land, to breathe, to face the growing
light of dawn with the sun behind;
the horizon unfurls before your
stretching limbs, before your
unshakable belief: nothing
will ever hold you fast again.

I like how feminist author and media scholar Susan
Douglas writes about Mary Beath as belonging to a "tradition
. . . of keen-eyed, gutsy women who have bound themselves to
the southwest," expressing for men and women alike "our
desires for love and liberation, and how the land . . . if we
watch closely, offers us metaphors for both." Beath is an
award-winning environmental illustrator, artist and activist,
whose political savvy has helped galvanize opposition to
industrial depredations in wilderness areas and reckless devel-
opments ruining small communities in urban landscapes. Her
hikes alone in the wildernesses of New Mexico, Arizona,
Colorado, Utah, and Wyoming have inspired the imagina-
tions of many women in the West.

In the poem "Cougar," Beath writes about the refuge of
freedom, amazement, and awareness even as the impersonal
danger of a predator's hunger moves unseen and not far away.

You walked step by even step, alone
on the trail until I found your tracks,

deer sometimes crossing uphill or down,
but never boldly treading
the open path. You: certain, easy,
maybe watching me. I thought not—the
inside of your tracks had iced over, a day
old, at least—but then I saw my
own bootprints had the same icy glaze. . . .
I stopped when I saw your tracks came
toward me downhill, but had also reversed—
you stepped precisely into each print, moving
the same way as me, up toward the sun.
Frightened then, I fled.

As the poems in *Refuge of Whirling Light* make clear, Beath's openness to the world includes the reader in an intimate conversation about what it means to be alive on this planet of risk and limits, a place in which to know one's own strength is as liberating as knowing one's own boundaries is empowering. Her poems have the gait of narrative that allows readers to think quietly and clearly about what she presents from her attentive observations of reality. As philosopher Martha Nussbaum, in her book *Poetic Justice*, observes "storytelling and literary imagination are not opposed to rational argument," but can, in fact, become "essential ingredients" in a clear-eyed view of the contradictions, tragedies, and feedbacks of living in the world. And storytelling is not opposed, either, to the Orphic and ecstatic that allows poetry to see and say human truths as no other medium can. Beath's native power of language gives poetic form to that sense of awe that led philosophy to evolve into the physical sciences, driven as much by a wonder at the marvels of creation as by a curiosity to make sense of how they work.

Beath's background as a student of biology at Duke, an art student at the Rhode Island School of Design, and a tutor of English in Turkey, coupled with her interests in complexity theory and her years as a naturalist, writer, and poet, as a designer for *Artforum* magazine in New York and an environmental artist-educator working on projects that range from the BLM's national monuments across the West to Grand Canyon habitat preservation, give her the confidence to move with ease through scholarly specialties and skills that can be intimidating.

Beath has arranged this collection of poems so a reader's attention can range through an open field of interlocking perspectives and preoccupations—from conversational poems that allow us to travel along with her through wild and human landscapes; to exploratory poems about a primordial relationship between Hermes, the Greek god of travelers and explorers in both physical and mental terrains, Athena the goddess of self-reliance and intrepid practicality, and Aphrodite the goddess of love; to poems about the ecologies of human relationships and the wilderness of emotion; to a final sestina, "Along the Rio Chama," a formal poetic cascade that takes the reader through the rapids of an invisible turbulence that follows in the wake of the poet's comfort with reality in all its confusions, beauties, and torments.

In the Rio Chama sestina, she writes:

What incendiary secrets smolder like underground coal fires in the raven
Night, where owl wings flash darkness across the stars and I swallow
An ancient unease that has curled along my spine like a whelk's expanding spiral?
What cycling tension propels our inner helical fires, the molecular spiral
Spring we share with down-drifting detritus of ancient seas, the bones
Of these hills now thinly covered in dry skins of grass and sage?
No answer. But this: You have followed the contours of this land as carefully as the raven
Maps a cliff edge. You have dabbed the river's mud, word by word,
     as persistently as the swallow
Has made her rock-protected nest. You have ridden the invisible turbulence.
Rested before continuing his survey of the river's watershed. The turbule

This first book of Mary Beath's poems has, for me, that

haunting intimacy and clarity of feeling that environmental activist Joanna Macy once expressed in the title of her book *World as Lover, World as Self*. Without clouding sentiment, but with heartfelt welcoming, Beath witnesses the natural world, from which humans have never been exiled, with the same open and appreciative attention one gives to children, lovers, beloved spouses, animal friends, and transformative insights and ideas.

In her invocation to Hermes, written in the remote Ojitos Canyon north of Santa Fe, Beath recollects her encounter with the famous statue of the Roman Hermes, Mercury, in the fountain in the National Gallery's marble hall,

a Mercury bronzed in winged
sandals, winged hat—narrow contrivances meant
to catch your wiliness and motion. Guide me.
You're never clear, you never fail to make a leap.
Open me to energies that liven the wind, these
dancing green stalks, these water striders riding
the surface of air and water, at home only
where the two meet. Now you see them, now they're
gone, their shadows sliding over the pool's sand
bottom. Water, light, sun, night. The underworld,
the overworld, the worlds unseen, your strange, precise
guidance. . . . Keep me
clear about what I'm doing, but not so clear
I'm rigid. Loose. Quicksilver and fleet. Practical
and completely gratuitous, like the color of this
butterfly, the perfect gifts from nowhere.
Bless me. Bless us all.

The poems of *Refuge of Whirling Light* radiate with fearlessness and strength. Mary Beath sees human emotion and the natural world as radically the same, each at its core unencumbered by inhibition, self-consciousness, and neurosis *if* hearts are not closed to love and minds are not closed to nuance by the rigidity of dogma and the chains of control. Beath's poems are traveling companions for those of us who seek the liberating possibilities of an openness to the world exactly as it is, uncensored by expectations, real and mysterious beyond manipulation, free of the traps of easy safety and ignorant complacency, waiting for us to rejoice in it, and rejoin it on our own. ☙

—V. B. Price
September 2004

introduction

One bright winter afternoon in the ranching plains east of New Mexico's Manzano Mountains, I was bumping down an empty washboarded road in my pickup when an unlikely sign appeared. It stood at the entrance to a smaller dirt road, no buildings visible across the nearly flat fields. In peeling paint, it read: *Refuge of Whirling Light.* My first thought was, "Only in New Mexico! It's always been filled with whirling light and people ready to make some use of it." By that time I'd lived in New Mexico for more than ten years. One friend later suggested the Refuge might be connected to the Sufis and their retreat center in the Manzano's foothills, and reminded me of their focus on light and circling dances. That may be so, but I've never been able to find the sign again, nor any reference to the Refuge. The sign had been a stranger's quirky gesture, but it seemed emblematic. To me the words mean two things. First, a refuge where light whirls must promise a haven which both protects and opens to unexpected possibilities. Second, the spinning, unbridled light (wild freedom) is offered a place of safety, a resting place where the light itself can perhaps find a temporary form, or many forms, unpremeditated convergences of words. A form where, at least for a time, it belongs.

These same sensations—of freedom and belonging, of encountering the unexpected—have always drawn me to wander the land, especially alone. I understand now that writing gives me much the same nourishment. On walks as a child, when I was lucky, I'd feel relieved of all human-contrived constrictions, simultaneously tiny and enormous, with no need to explain myself or to fit anyone's categories. At the same time, my body seemed to resonate with an all-encompassing order. Yet I didn't need that sense of a larger pattern to find comfort, expansion, delight, and a measure of revelation—revelation that had nothing to do with God or religion. Freedom leads to the possibility of uncoerced belonging, and both provide the ease which allows an openness through which something new or the unexpected—or grace—can enter.

Early in my life I always lived within a few hours of the Atlantic, so at first my favorite places to wander were by the sea, with its expanses and movement. One fall on a coastal Maine island after a storm I came upon hundreds of tiny yellow warblers resting exhausted, low in dark spruces, blown off course during their migration. Grandfather's beard draped the branches around the hot loci of life, survivors of an extreme trial. The blinking, disoriented birds—puffed feathery spheres—had found momentary refuge. Long before I came upon the sign for the whirling light's refuge, I imagined those packets of living energy whirling in the hurricane, and by luck reaching a safe haven. Yards away, gale-driven breakers marked the edge of the hidden deep, its surface reflecting the bright low clouds like dancing mercury.

Then, in my mid-thirties, I found myself in the Southwest. Space seemed to stretch forever in the desert's clear, dry air: the landscape opened, and so did my inner world. Distances became vast; every idea, emotion, activity became richer. Since then, my life has been permeated by travels in the wilds of New Mexico, Arizona, Utah, Colorado, and Wyoming. Sometimes I go with friends, but most often I still hike alone. I'm partly attracted by the enlivening risk, partly curious of what I might discover on my own. I start with a tentative agenda, but always I'm surprised by the unexpected, the unplanned.

One day, I'd been walking for several hours in dusty hills above the Chama River, picking my way among scattered sand sage and snakeweed and a plant I didn't know with tiny blue-violet flowers. Heading back to my truck I began to follow a dry arroyo, which twisted and deepened until its crumbling sandy sides reached twenty feet, straggly roots hanging forlornly from eroded vertical banks. Suddenly I smelled wet air. The smell grew stronger until I rounded a corner and found myself in a fecund, lush grove. Its spongy grass-covered floor was fed by a hidden seep, as different from the parched surrounding hillsides as possible. Water—life—from dry ground. As with the warblers on the coast, the metaphors were multiple. The clearest was that life—any creative act—can emerge like a spring in the most unlikely spots. In a few feet the seep became a lively shallow stream. Down the drainage the water was channeled into the local *acequia*, irrigating gardens and fields, then joining the desert river.

Writing gives me the same sense of exploration, of crossing boundaries, of bumping into the marvelous—or at least the unforeseen. I seek, and often find, freedom from my own entrenched thought patterns. Poet Jane Hirshfield speaks of "threshold consciousness," a liminal state, the mind's equivalent of edges in ecosystems, exceptionally fertile zones where land meets sea, or the bosque along the Rio Grande becomes dryer ground. Dawn or dusk. "[Threshold consciousness] is, like the act of writing itself, about stepping past what we already think we know and into an entirely new relationship with the many possibilities of being, with the ultimately singular and limitless mystery of being. Above all, it is about freedom, and the affection for all existence that only genuine freedom brings."

When I venture alone into the wild, I don't leave myself behind, but enter an enlarged context. When I explore with words, I don't abandon conscious thought, but release narrow control so that language can expand its territory. In *The Forgotten Language, Contemporary Poets and Nature*, editor Christopher Merrill says, "Language, like nature, is an order larger than any individual; poets surrender to that order, hoping to discover in the process meanings they were not aware of when they sat down to write. The same may hold for their experience of the wild." For me, that variety of experience *began* in the wild.

Beyond language and nature, there is another resonance across categories. The body/mind's own wilderness of love and sexuality moves past tight geometries of rationality into a fuller realm, a realm more tuned to the rest of creation.

These poems are an outgrowth of an attitude: we needn't compartmentalize our experiences, sequestering nature from human sensuality, from emotion, from language, from ideas. This is not a new perspective, especially in poetry. I also share another understanding with many writers: although the natural world offers rich metaphors for human concerns, we must not deny its separate reality. The exhausted yellow warblers quivered in those dark spruces for their own survival, not simply as a compelling metaphor for me. I also acknowledge my debts to Surrealist experiments in automatic writing, and to the many poets who have written about nature, themselves, and all fellow creatures.

In her essay, "Winter Hours," poet Mary Oliver describes a familiar sensation: "Stepping out into the world, into the grass, onto the path, was always a kind of relief. I was not escaping anything. I was returning to the arena of delight. I was stepping across some border. I don't mean that the world changed on the other side of the border, but that I did, too. . . . I could not be a poet without the natural world. Someone else could. But not me." Nor me.

These poems arrived almost through the back door. Their meanings and rhythms grew from a place neither mediated by self-consciousness nor framed by my own expectations. Nearly every morning soon after dawn for several years, I'd make a cup of tea, sit down at my writing table, and fill one page of a green 6 x 9" spiral notebook. Then I'd close the cover, usually not even reading through what I'd written for several days. Writing these words was more like priming the pump for other tasks. As the weeks and months passed with notebooks filling, I became even less concerned with what happened with any particular day's first page. I simply let go. The process wasn't exactly automatic writing, since I did pause to mull over what flowed from my pen. Once the first lines made it out, often triggered by what I could see of my garden or what rested on my deep adobe window sill, an idea would kick in and spin itself out. I was aware when the end of the page approached, but rarely needed to take firmer control to wrap it up. Many days the pieces were abysmal, but as frequently a complete whole emerged.

After several months I began to call the daily poems *efful - gences*. I had to check the dictionary to confirm it was a real word. Yes. *Radiant splendor*. A little high flown, but that *is* what the morning poems felt like. They seemed to radiate from some bright inner source even when their content was dark. In no other part of my creative life have I been so consistently in touch with something beyond my rational mind, that part of awareness and goad to action which has various names: the unconscious, the muse, daimon, archetype, perhaps even spirit. Between sleeping and full wakefulness—that liminal state—as the tea's caffeine began to buzz in my system, these words strung themselves together more informed by dreams, shadowy emotions, memory, and obscure wisdom than thought. Mary Oliver again: "What I hear is almost a voice. . . . Every poet knows it. . . . One hopes for gifts. One hopes for direction. It is both physical, and spooky. It is intimate and inapprehensible."

Though these poems started as pieces only for myself, after I began reading them to friends the idea of putting a group together into a book began to grow. Some of these poems are barely edited, copied directly from those green notebooks, but others needed more tinkering. Still, I tried not to clean up the freshness from those early mornings.

My conscious concerns surfaced frequently in the effulgences, but with the prisms of understanding and expression tilted. The book's organization loosely follows these themes.

Over and over I returned to the opening and pure pleasure of remaking my life in New Mexico's high desert—an ongoing enterprise many have shared. I'd changed my place on the map, but "the map is not the territory," as Gregory Bateson once famously quoted the scientist and writer Alfred Korzybski. Ground truth—the territory—is in individual stories, others' idiosyncrasies illuminating our selves like reflected light. Science offers a particular variety of story, often purporting to be a map so accurate no territory could possibly rebel. I know this intimately, since I count among my official credentials a degree in zoology from Duke and many years working in natural history forums from exhibit design to posters to books to essays and poetry. Regardless of its limitations, science offers a seductive way to organize the world. Survival strategies, metabolic pathways, and neurophysiology, for example, can be as sensual to me as any references to mystery. Another of my official credentials is a degree in fine arts from the Rhode Island School of Design, a place where I fled when science's seductions began to change in my mind to gripping, binding cords. Visual art has required me to pay even closer attention to the world's particularities than demanded by science, with its focus on repeatability and patterns.

The first three sections loosely explore place, and story melded to place, following my own tales or threads from others' lives.

The short section of three invocations nods to the archetypal world of ancient Greece, revived in the psychologies of Carl Jung, James Hillman, Ginette Paris, and others. Human characteristics and aspirations can be abstracted in order to be discussed coherently, but in the gods they are reinvigorated with human complexity, embodied in a way that I now find indispensable.

As in my conscious life, some days I focused on the way the internal emotional world mirrors the fluid and complex workings of ecosystems, rife with relationship, non-linearity, and feedback loops. And vice versa. Fusing love and sex with the natural world gave me some distance from my heart's flailings, provided solace, and often illuminated things that had been opaque. Simultaneously I felt a deeper involvement with the world beyond human affairs, my own sensations of desire or despair braided together with the facts of the land: wind, singing frogs, storms, changing light.

The fifth section ventures more directly into the sexual wilderness. The sixth and seventh sections are love poems—or anti-love poems—about two different love affairs.

Finally, the Coda is not an effulgence, but a sixteenth century poetic form called a sestina. The sestina's loose formality gave me a chance to use structure to build a sense of place, ordering with language a landscape I've wandered many times in many seasons, filled with questions, filled with desire and delight. Ezra Pound once said, "The sestina is like a thin sheet of flame, folding and infolding upon itself." A refuge for whirling light. ◉

—Mary Beath
May 2004

Section 1

Refuge
of
Whirling
Light

Cougar

You walked the same
snowy paths, low and silent,
color of dried bigtooth maple leaves
still clinging like decorations to the
open thicket, short trunks dark against snow.
You walked step by even step, alone
on the trail until I found your tracks,
deer sometimes crossing uphill or down,
but never boldly treading
the open path. You: certain, easy,
maybe watching me. I thought not—the
inside of your tracks had iced over, a day
old, at least—but then I saw my
own bootprints had the same icy glaze.
Cold. Cleanness to match dryness,
enclosed forest, open and bright, snow
like light from earth, forest
illuminated from its floor. A few
rabbit tracks, but mostly you, lean
and strong, eyes peering ahead, ears
twitching, tail long and gently curved.
The maples arched partway over the
trail, a squirrel chattered.
High peeps like a swarm of insects
surrounded me once, almost too high for
birds, short and sharp and incandescent.

I stopped when I saw your tracks came
toward me downhill, but had also reversed—
you stepped precisely into each print, moving
the same way as me, up toward the sun.
Frightened then, I fled.
Down from the snow I drove east,
away from the mountain trail.
A masked osprey watched, alert and
ready on a cottonwood's crown, nearly
drowned in golden winter quiet.
I fled down a straight, washboarded
road, empty of all but sagging fences
and a single painted sign:
Refuge of Whirling Light. ๑

Crossing

Thread through lashed-together
fissioning scenes, make your way
through chaos held like
rocks in a rapid, not held in
lockstep to fit according to plan, but
still held inside an outer boundary. Now.
Step through.
Start at one side, step in
and find a route through—because
no way around exists—you must get
across the rapid, you must
watch where you're going, feel with your
body as if you were blind, but not
give up your sight—you need
everything you have to not flip
on the rocks, to not become part
of the tumbling mess, to not
become only a shard
in the fragmented landscape.
One step.
One step more
and I halt as if at a
threshold I can't cross;
going in or going out I can't tell.

The abstracted world does not matter
when the only way through is one
step and one step more, the
strap on my left sandal rubbing
my inner ankle. I think I hesitate
in going forward, but I wonder if I
never slow enough to grasp the present.
Can that be? I need to tune my step to
the swirling illusions; but they *must* have
solid cores. Do they change any more than
rapids over hard rock? Standing waves.
I have halted. Know this:
threshold is not wall.
It is only one ripple.
One ripple in the larger pattern.
Cross. ☙

Solid Ground

1

Yellowstone, 1989

The definition of earth grew
past all guarantees.
Beneath scattered spruce the ground
had melted to a slurried mocha ring;
at its fluid center, bubbles
erupted in digestive gurgles,
popping as they crested
viscous interfaces, releasing
gas in satisfying low sounds,
as sweaty bodies suck
against each other and slide free.
I stared, I listened, I felt
the solid ground under me
become less solid, certainty
turn around: sometime I would step
and the earth would fall away beneath
me, no longer able to support my abundant
animal weight.

When I had my fill I made my way
back across the summer meadow,
skirting the dozen grazing buffalo,
paused again beside a round channel
to a lower world. A hot spring steamed next
to bistort and daisies, water as clear
as the mud had been opaque. Along its margins
lay bleached bones from a buffalo, spit out
after her winter meat had been cooked off.
She'd stepped unaware into an opening,
the earth falling away. Her skull was missing,
her pelvis gone, but I furtively gathered
one hump vertebrae, its upper process
longer than my forearm.
Its form stroked my sense of shape; but more
than artifact I craved a talisman
for the day
the earth would fall away
with no warning
from my prancing
heedless
animal weight. ☙

Solid Ground

2

Toroweap, 2000

From three thousand feet straight
down, the river growled.
At an airy distance we watched
the rafts and kayaks, tiny humans
scouting Lava Falls: how best to
challenge death and live? For an
hour they read the flow and plotted,
then one by one slid down the
left-hand tongue, all safe but one.
That raft, the smallest, flipped.
But the roiling hole disgorged them:
upended boat with oarsman clinging
to its bottom.

Three strangers watched beside me.
They radiated strain: a family, perhaps,
in mourning, with that familiarity and hush.

Later the eldest of the strangers
told me this: for twenty years his quiet
daughter lived in Fairbanks but had moved
back home. Camping alone one long
summer's day, she'd strolled along
a glacial river. With no warning, the bank
gave way. The icy flow swept her to
roadless ground, beyond a shout, the
river's growl too loud. For eleven days
she lived on berries, in jeans and
jacket. A river trip saw her at a
distance, someone stumbled on her
car, then finally they found her.

We all watched the wet ribbon below.
Once she asked her chatty Dad, "How cold's
the water?" With binoculars we followed
the capsized boat until a kayak
caught it and brought it safe to shore.
After dinner I joined them, and we talked of
places to hike, ruins, fires, flying.
She stayed mostly silent,
taken once,
and returned. &

Go West

Moving west from here the land opens,
climbs from the river's folded valley to
distances where undulations painted
with greasewood and saltbush rise suddenly
to rock mesas: the road cuts straight
across one just beyond the
Rio Puerco. Even speeding through at
seventy, the space embraces, the space
swallows your speed, the space makes you
understand how small you are, the space
makes you understand you *ARE*.
I set out west one June morning at dawn,
sun at my back, full moon
straight ahead. Nothing more profound
than possibility, the inner beat inscribed:
GO WEST. Accidents of history: humans clumped
like kudzu in the east. Accidents of
geology: because earth turns the way it
turns, bunched mountains facing into ocean
capture rain, dry these rough expanses.
Yet lack of intent matters little to the
heart's response: to open. To open like
the land, to breathe, to face the growing
light of dawn with sun behind;
the horizon unfurls before your
stretching limbs, before your
unshakable belief: nothing
will ever hold you fast again. ◉

One April

I'd rolled my bag out
by Echo Amphitheatre
and could just see Abiquiu Lake,
the Sangre de Christos behind,
Pedernal to the right. At dawn I turned
over to a sky ablaze, deep
orange, alive. Not the burning
bush, the burning sky.
Could I make a life here?
The show slowly faded, running
through its tricks.
Never will the sky hold still.

The last paintings I saw
before I left NY for good
were careful square canvases,
head size, of the night skies
over Santa Fe: a little land, clouds
hiding moon, edges lit like
flowing memories, diffuse and
sharp at once, the clouds
clouds, the sky
sky, the space
space, each small painted
square a frozen night, caught,
captured
from the living flux.
They made me feel my hunger. ✆

Abiquiu

Choose colors for Abiquiu, where the
sherbet cliffs watch over sage, over
the river, over the highway, over the
Presbyterians pursuing spiritual renewal
or weaving skills, where the sky's blue
anchors the land in an upending of
gravity, where one early Easter morning
I looked out over glowing grama
grasses to see a white horse galloping
toward me, backlit with mane alive with wind,
haloed with a white hot sun. Choose colors.
Ochre, maroon, the orange of cantaloupe but
paler and pinker, dark eggplant for
shadows under piñon where the desert
cottontails wait, yellow-green of
young cottonwood leaves, pale
creamy yellow which becomes blinding
at midday, rock that rubs away to sand
at a brush of your hand. Polished black
of beetle back, golden yolk of desert marigold,
of pollen from prickly pear or brief penstemon,
the golden yolk of your heart, filled with
light, filled with colors unchosen,
unbidden, unmatchable, filled with
space enclosed, ready to break open
to break into a thousand cliffs, a
thousand cliff swallows, a thousand
unnamed lives dashing past in the
moonlit night where everything glows
black and silver, colorless and vibrant. ◉

Fullness / Emptiness

Fullness can be like emptiness:
so extreme nothing emerges as pattern or
as detail, the fullness as spacious
as any emptiness, its clinging uproar
the foam of a wave, only fizz,
wind with no direction, wind dense
with spirits, memories, forgotten
sentences, with only disconnected words
flying in the mists. In the primal
beginning all existed as potential,
nothing more—but *nothing more*
was everything. This fullness is bounded,
is in my mind, recurs often, ready with
potential swirling in the mists. And
does the fullness, ready with potential,
need to be ripe to begin shaking out its
details, its stories, one by one, simple or
complex? Or is it *not* the fullness's
ripeness, its time-fed growth, that
finally elaborates the patterns, but the
calm and focused gaze I cast
on it which gives it leave to become
a world, to sing its stories color by curve,
green by down on cheek, honey flame
lighting beeswax by worn moose tooth
still resting in its bleached jawbone? ◉

Distant

Distant. As far as the western rim of
the Grand Canyon is from tourists peering
over from the paved lot at Grand View; as far
as both are from the cold river at the bottom.
Distant. As far as the redtail from the vole,
the osprey from the cutthroat trout, the winter
sun from iris blossoms. Distant. As far as
my hand from a cat's paw, today from next month,
love from silence. Distant. As far as the dry
leafless shore from the anemones and octopus
and jeweled blennies in the wet saltiness
of the Sea of Cortez.

Not distant is drowning: off the shore, all
fears realized: falling from the rim, body broken
on every tilted bench, every rocky outcrop; taken
by another's story, no way back to your own,
nothing of your own left; no breath, no
breathing. Drowning: the justification of
distance. In some blind narrow world, only
these two exist: to keep to the shore or to be
submerged and die.
But to dive in and not drown is to swim.

When I was seven I took swimming lessons
at the Y in a cold, dim, chlorine-smelly pool
echoing with calls of a dozen other girls.

My mother, terrified, watched from wooden bleachers.
She didn't swim and wanted me to learn, so I
would never drown. More: so I would never
fear drowning. She didn't know how
much she trained me for, couldn't see
how my shivering and my blue lips, my gasping
for air and my side stroke would finally let
me kick out, paddle away, would save
me not only from drowning but from her
own distance, her own land-bound, careful,
unwished distance. ☉

Walking By Water

I found the peacock feathers on the ditch
last spring, remains of a coyote's dinner.
Plumes, no eyes. They lean over my files,
their shafts white, their dark
fronds hanging down. I hear
the peacocks call by Los Poblanos
barn, high and longing. They wander
the land, the ditch banks, strutting,
mating, ornaments alive and curious.
I hear them call, like aching women
or lost shades, when I've been
walking the ditches, peeking into
rich folks' back yards, watching
crows. I've walked by water and
have eased, always, from how I started.
The mountains loom east, the light catches
red willow branches, water moves in and
out of shadow, a redtail circles, kestrels
call, brittle cochea still spreads
its seed. I greet the black dog Nula
through her fence, rub her ears, think
how she's named Penula for the silkies
off the Irish coast, the seals who raise
their dark heads from the cold sea, curious.
Nula licks my hand.

I think of her owner, with my name, who
swims alone for eight hours, ten hours,
across lakes, across bays; who treads
water in the pool to keep in shape.
Nula presses her soft side hard against
the fence and watches me as I
walk away. ☙

Cascades

Yesterday a Cooper's hawk lounged
on a fence post by the ditch, made
a few small nasal quacks, milder than
a duck's honks, too cartoony for his fierce
attention. I noted him because I'd never
seen a Cooper's here: the unavoidable draw
of the unusual, the new. It pulls me the
way a smooth white stone calls out
among fractured sharp grey ones. I know
the admonition to love the ordinary.
I do: the willows greening out, the
deep magenta plum leaves against
warm adobe walls, the apple blossoms
scenting air, the motion of light in water.
But attention requires more: it requires
sensing the patterns composed of
known ordinary, no matter how luscious, how
plain, and noting how the ever moving pattern
changes. Or suddenly includes a new piece:
the Cooper's hawk, with his stubby wings
for maneuvering between trees in his song-bird
chases. He belongs here as much as the kestrel,
or the redtail, or the blue grosbeak who he'd
happily tear to shreds for dinner. But for the
moment, he's new; the bosque cascades
with his presence.
Any life would. ✆

1.1.2000

From a distance a faint low thrum;
above the trees an incandescent
disturbance; they rose; their sound
grew as they flew toward us, against
the pre-dawn grey the birds still dark
separated into curtains close overhead
sliding across each other: deafening,
blinding; they swept over, back, around,
raucous; snow geese, thousands.
They settled again in the shallow
water just in front among stilted
cranes whose heads still lay across their
backs. Asleep. The light rose, the geese
became a huge white raft, drinking,
preening, fidgeting. The cranes, one by one
began to purl their bird words, stepping
through the water. And at once the
geese rose, a sound like a sudden
cataract, deep, wing beats; like a
massive wind through forest, but
lower, blotting out everything, their
wing rush becoming again high
garooos. Off to the right another flock
lifted with the same deep whoosh.
A celebration? A celebration.
A celebration *every* morning. ☉

Ice

Quiet but for low shushings of wind,
downy woodpecker intent on ponderosa
trunk, and open clefts in ice. Three feet
down, past smoothed frozen layers the
creek's water still flows and sings
upward with a hollow gurgling and
high splash at once. Weighted
stillness and calm of standing
firs. Solid, gravity vast. Grey
white frozen water where the surface
has thawed—frozen—thawed—frozen—
spread in monochrome grace. Silent.
Beneath the spruce by the bridge,
mica-thin crystals grow like
minerals, regular but not regular.
A high, delicate tink, crunch,
tink tink when they shatter. They've
broken, but not broken, just rearranged
themselves; and if not broken, then next
week, or the next, they will melt back
to the racing stream that's never,
all the icy winter,
stopped. ◎

Branches hazed with buds, elms clad
in tiny wings, green and set to fly;
willows greenest, but still pale,
thin, only promising—
latticework filling out
cell by cell, photon by photon,
light waving with the wind.
Their roots aren't angry at the
dry ground, the winter as warm
as most springs. They pump away,
concentrating what they find,
shutting down whole sections,
rootlets shriveled and abandoned.
Buds swell while moon wanes.
Barely visible tree haze thickens
denser daily and sap flows
upward with no heart to pump it,
drawn instead by outward reach,
capillary crawl, and osmotic
orientations up. And out.
They make their own stationary fog,
a mist which thickens as it stands
from breath to scrim, from scrim to
body, articulated leaf by leaf by leaf.
But that's still to come.
Today I see only promise,
delicate as memory,
certain as imagination. ☙

Human stories roll across the
landscape, demanding attention, voicing
their energy, responding to my questions;
the land only vibrates in the wind.
Or not. Rocks and lava, caught in the moment
of fall, of flow, expose fractured
innards and cooled heat, vibrate only rarely.
These human voices and the tales they tell
deflect with their looks, their gestures,
their act of giving me what I can feel
myself, or at least understand. I can't
put myself in the piñon's place, trembling at
the edge, growing at the upper end of a
human-sized bowl, the lower end a slot I peer
through to see the river's ribbon, its white-flecked
trail through the deepest cleft of all. I can't
know the piñon's mind, though I try.
These tales from another's mouth make sense,
but spread a thin veneer over all the
rest. Still, the distraction is never
irredeemable: the human voices go, the wind
comes forward again, blows the chittering,
zooming swifts; the piñon watches the same
stretch of river through its rock cleft,
watches the tiny rafts with their human cargo
pass beneath it, all stories quieted,
distance far too deep. ☙

Hard Frost

The serrano leaves aren't
nipped, though I harvested all their
red and green hotness last night.
My yard's protected, warmer than
the open land around your
plants, warmer than the sweeps
along the west mesa where the
chill moves across the ground with
no rocks, no adobe walls toasted
by the sun to warm the night. My
yard *must* be the place of
choice—protected, enclosed,
temperatures modulated,
violets nestled under cherry tree,
small lawn soft and cool. But I
know I'd rather roam the mesas,
open to sky, open to whipping wind,
open to space in all directions,
skin not enclosed, not enclosing,
but dissolving to icy air, to
stars, to dark distances
I can't see, but can feel as if
they were my fingers' tips. ☺

Gordian Knot

Gordian knot: a problem insoluble on its
own terms. Conundrum: a problem
whose solution is a pun. Idea: what
language comes to sometimes, but not
what triggers words. Problem: a tension
implying a change which will reduce
the tension and open other possibilities.
Tension: two or more elements tending to
move differently, held together by an
invisible, mysterious force. Tension: a
question with no apparent answer.
Tension: a question with an answer
which is obscure. Tension: expectation
unfulfilled. Tension: risk. Tension:
muscles working against gravity.
Tension: where two substances of different
viscosities meet, the surface of a stream,
the reason for water striders. Tension:
where different desires meet. Tension:
where the same desires meet. Tension:
the force that finally opens the
milkweed pod and sprays its
downy seeds into autumn air.
Tension: the answer without a question.
Tension: the head of a drum, the
string on a cello, the pull of the
horizon, the lift of wind under a
hawk's wing, the desire that propels
you forward, the desire that keeps your
rhythms not quite in synch with the world. ◉

A Map Trick

See yourself drive
on narrow black top or
washboarded dirt
rolling across country
on a plane of existence
that needs no muscles,
imagine the distance
you can cover, mountain
range by mesa, river by dam,
truck stop by chapter house,
dust by tree, always space
and light, time passing.
You know it will be.
You chart your route.
It's not terra incognita
except for your particular
passage through it. This
time, next time. The hours
pass, your eyes follow the
horizon as it turns to hills,
rocky outcrops, sage flats,
gas stations, dumped pickups,
grazing sheep, three clouds,
baking heat, a brief storm—
none of those details show up
on any map,
all those details more important
than the road—*except*
the road leads in
the road leads on. ❧

Racing Home

Virgas, first far off and grey, caught me
in swirling whiteouts. Fifty miles of
Straight Cliffs alternated dark and snowy
filo layers ending at Navajo Mountain's
smooth blue breast. Piñon hillsides greyed
to monochrome with thin washes of ice
on every needle and branch; snow fog
drifted at the edge of Black Mesa.
Lake Powell had turned the color of glacier milk,
but greener, with surf like Maine's coast
under sand-storm black skies, alcoves
carving themselves deeper, wind and sand
scouring off grains by the fist-full.

I'd had enough of April winter
and raced my truck toward home.

Three deer paused by the road
in half light, their bodies the color
of clouds and rain. The first moved
just fast enough to miss my front bumper;
the other two, with some animal wisdom
wiser than my own dash,
waited, still, as the roadside
grasses whipped in the wind around
their delicate ankles, and
I sped past. ๑

At the Edge, Overlooking the Paria, 3,000 Feet Down, Winding Eight Miles to the Colorado

Watch the piñon and the raven and the
water grey and cold far below.

The bonsai piñon, old but two feet tall,
offers this: if you live where ground
gives way, on soil less soil than rock,
grow slowly, don't
outstrip your nourishment.

The raven alone in updrafts beside
red walls offers this: if you're
curious, the land will never
disappoint you and the young condors
will take *you* as *their* teacher.

The Paria's water, grey and cold,
offers this: lesson one: move.
You will work on rock the way
rock lets itself be worked, and it will
be taken away, grain by grain, and your
work will make a canyon never imagined.
But once alive in the world, the canyon
will be known as an unmatched wonder,
solid and mysterious.

And the canyon? The canyon will teach
curve and layer and wind sign and
mud bank and distant strip of
blue and flood and
stillness and
time. ❀

A Companionable Obsession

Two times must run side by side, out of
sync: what happens in this time has
already happened in that other time.
Sometimes. My father's broken pocket
watch hangs on the wall
attaching one moose jawbone to
its mirror image. A still photo
works when it implies the past,
implies the future, offers a bridge
between. A friend once looked at me in
dismay: "You have no clocks in your house!"
But the clock hums, the wheels whir,
inner time tracks the sun, adrenals
stir every two hours even in sleep, ovaries
pop eggs in cycles said to match the
moon, but rarely do in living women, skin
begins to resemble preserved leather, supple but
creased with use. The clivia growing by my table
with her blooming helmet of tangerine
trumpets follows an unknown chronometer.

I measure days in words, in lines, in
colors, in conversations, in pages; as
they drift into the distance, only rough
shapes remain. But within those shapes
limbs and animals reach out—hands and
snakes, say—as present as this moment.
They reach beyond me into the other time,
the time which lies ahead, full,
already building like an August cloud
against limitless space. ๑

The Box

The box: squared off, structured to
hold in, hold out, immobile, linear,
rigid, not prone to morphing. Or maybe
it *can* morph past its cardboard
limits, its framed-up, mitred, pegged,
nailed, unbending joints. Especially its
joints. Joints: places where the culture's
structures can be broken, where
Loki lives, where coyote pops out, where
Hermes finds the openings
to escape and bring us with him.
Great alarm. At the box, at the joints,
at the non-linear, at the unexpected. Our
skins are permeable, our minds more permeable.
Follow another's story, follow your own.
It is not the same. It *is* the same.
Follow lives written in a stack of
bound paper less than a foot square, and
understand lives revealed in their own
writing, women finding the joints in their
boxes, climbing out, or morphing the
boxes they hadn't made. But sometimes those
boxes still held. What of the boxes
we make ourselves? So lovingly drilling
holes for the pegs, measuring, furnishing,
painting, not remembering to add enough
doors. Or remembering the doors. And windows.

Forgetting sometimes to open them, or
to know we can leave to take a walk, even if
we circle back. We can meander and
return to find the squared-off box
transformed into a pie tin
or yurt; or even into a cooling pool
deep in a shady glade. ☙

Three Cultures

Three cultures:
The blind,
the bombers, and
the land-besotted.

The blind could
as happily live in Memphis
or St. Pete, Fargo, or Missoula.

The bombers layer over this place of
obscurity, this odd outback, with
hives of physicists and secrets and F-18s,
even while it stays an odd outback.
The billboard north of town reads:
"Welcome to New Mexico, World Capital
of weapons of mass destruction," with
a mushroom cloud for art.

The land-besotted are the rest of us
who wake on summer mornings
and smell the cool night, who feel the
heat's clean arpeggios, who hear
the distances as if the desert
read aloud from its library of
rock and sage, turning pages
every hour, every day. ✆

Section 2

Off
the Map:
Ground
Truth I

Off Canyon Road, Santa Fe

The two empty houses rang
with past lives, their stone floors
sending back our voices, the inside adobe
walls half-repainted cloud white. The wooden
doors had all been made to order. Your aunt,
dead now for a dozen years, roamed the garden
and the buildings, sometimes happy, sometimes
not. Your uncle also lurked, in life a writer.
But failed, alas.
Across the covered swimming pool we could see
to Santa Fe Baldy, its late April snow
glowing. In the neglected garden a grape vine
had just leafed out, indomitable: your father
had brought it back fifty years before
from Afghanistan. In one corner of the
big house's only livable room sat an old
letter press, paint the color of oxidized
copper chipping from its heavy steel.
You said, "That's Gustave Baumann's.

Do you want it?" I held to it hard with
my right hand, feeling his long gone skills,
knowing the many woodcuts the press had
printed. Captured scenes: aspen bowers,
Taos dancers, Velarde orchards, enclosed
summer gardens. You told me tale after
tale: of the parties in the big room when
you were very young; of the publishing
company your aunt and uncle started in
NY; of the luminaries alert to
each other's angles; of your older son
whose fondness for grass fought with
his singing cello; of your younger son,
the blond Viking, who worked in metal and
threw runic bones with innocent hope
of foretelling the future. ◈

San Juan River

I

Unbinding, days building
on days, river banks on
river banks, 'til what we share
of wind and water, heat and
food rebinds us, but not
like loads strapped onto rafts,
but the way the silt binds
to flowing river, the river's
coils and riffles to the rocks, to
the canyon, to drops so
steep the water's surface tilts.
Down the river, eyes open, mouth
open, ears open, pores open to
every new turn, every ledge and
shift of light, every breath of
Russian olive nectar, sweet and
dark—to flower smell as thick
brown river is to mountain stream.
Open to sky, always wet or nearly so,
never far from river sound or mud
or sand, or blue-chinned lizards,
meditating to the rhythms that
made the canyons deep
and left nothing free of echoes
rumbling with long
slow breaking waves of time. ᕉ

San Juan River

II

Bring what's inside to the light,
what's far from skin and
make it yours, put together
memory's sheets with fragments
from the greater map. Avoid
the traps, it goes without saying,
shadows at the edge, the edges
stepping down, slowly as the
light moves, unfocused and
complete, then fades, shadows
rust, maroon, violet-blue, deep night blue,
cool against afternoon heat,
fractured at first like the rock, then
unbroken, still glowing with inner
buzz, reflected from walls still
in sun, from your inner eye, the
flashing water. In sun, in shadow,
bright, then soft, hot then cool then
hot. The canyon turns, the sun arcs,
you think of nothing, you think of
the blister on your fourth finger, you
think of asking how time can slow.
In light, in shadow, you watch the rocks. ◈

San Juan River

III

Once in the Met I saw a singing stone
strung up in a small shrine from
India or Tibet, behind glass,
the taped guide playing its
subtle note in my ear, out of
context, like all museum fare.
But the singing stones in the
grey rock bowl above the San Juan
lived neither in shrines nor behind
glass, lying scattered, camouflaged
above the river. They rang like bells
when we dropped them, miraculously
resonant, their tones reverberating in
the open rock room, a room worn by water,
carved by floods. Low, high, more muted or
clearer: they made a melodious percussion
set and we crouched with stones between
us and jammed, my water bottle a
deeper note. We'd suffered together under
a mutual gag order: a silence old and awkward
and pointless, grown from some obscure
misunderstanding. We laughed and gazed
around at the invisible sounds and
laughed some more, concentrating
on the music. The stones weren't mute,
yet neither did they speak in words,
but their voices eased us past our
silence, gave us back each other. ☙

Liminal Beings   39

My violin sits quietly under the
lip of my bench, its glowing wood
a sculpture, an exquisite flower:
hollow, beckoning. The green steamer
trunk sits upended in the shed: heavy
with photographs, with my mother's satin
wedding gown, with my grandfather's bible
inscribed "John Goodship Beath." I wanted them;
I don't know what to do with them. The photos
stare at me—or would if I pulled them
from their green metal box—sepia to
fading kodachrome. People who meant
a lot to me, or nothing at all, except as
some flowering of DNA partly matching
mine. They ask nothing, they
offer nothing, they exist only as I see
them—a reflection of my own searching
eyes. And the violin? Were I to play it
again, it would respond to my touch, but it
would answer with its own voice, a liminal being.
Do all things have their own voices, living
or not? We play them all, and they
sing to us in tune or not, depending on
our skill. Perhaps they sing past our skill
with melodies as alive as beating hearts,
as aware as eyes staring hard at a
camera's curved lens. ☙

Istanbul

Thirty years ago in Istanbul I
traveled ancient streets in a
red down jacket, hair long and light,
a foot taller than any of the men who
watched me, covert and curious, from under
flat woolen caps. All their women were
at home. Alone, I crossed the Bosphorus
on a crowded ferry to visit mosques and
museums, then churches made into one or
the other, all remaining art gouged clean
of eyes. I traveled by myself,
leaving my lover with his well-oiled
Hermes typing at our bright window on the
Bay of Fenerbaçe. I inhaled the
disturbing scent of the Levant, fecund and
exciting, wandered graveyards of centuries,
turban-topped stones tilting like
stout masts of slowly sinking ships. I learned
to count in Turkish, to buy vegetables and
cheese in daily markets, the old women all
amused and friendly. Once a Brit stopped me
on the street to ask if I would be
a movie extra: the land route to India
was still open and streamed with kids
my age, who searched and searched, often stoned,

as stunned as me by the world's unimagined
variety and strangeness. But I was young—
too young to do what I desired—to absorb
the place so I could make it into
art; young enough so it could make me into
someone I would not have become. Mosaic shards
turned to patterns in my blood, muezzin
calls at dawn reminded me of what I
could not reach, dolphins arcing past
the ferry's bow in the burnished
Golden Horn became a thread to Homer.
I began to know how accidental freedom—my
rare, uneasy freedom—not only let me
breathe, but bound me tight to
freedom's gift:
possibility. ✆

Haystack Summer

On my wall hang two cast paper sculptures
pulled from the same plaster mold one
summer on the coast of Maine: one
stark pulp white, the other mottled grey
tinted with powdered pigment. They
slide down the wall in a disoriented
cresting wave, and after three narrow feet
break off abruptly to a flat, angled-up square.
The potter who coached me through
making molds, starting with a clay form, was
a dowdy woman, mid-life, half the clay team,
very skilled, even famous, but
taciturn and uncomfortable. She felt
besieged by eager students who had
access to her from dawn to midnight.
Their straws in her solar plexus sucked
too much of her juice. She felt drained dry,
she could barely show up for demonstrations.
I meant my pair of paper waves as
explorations of an idea: the white one elegant
and lovely, the dark I tried to make "ugly,"

leaving roughness, dingy soot suggestions, not
pretty. Unsurprisingly, their flowing forms won
out. No matter what the surface or my idea
of "ugly," the dark paper shape hung regally next
to its mate, a study in variation, only, or
twos—the dark and light—no hint of
ugliness at all. I tried to talk to the
shut-down potter about my effort to make
"ugly," and its failure, wanting
words with her beyond recipes for plaster
casting. She heard me out, but nothing in
my question or my brittle paper forms
tripped a switch. She nodded, unsmiling, not
intrigued, not tempted, "It's something for you
to pursue," she said, neutral as unformed
clay. And she moved on, in a holding pattern
until her obligations ended and she could flee. ☙

Breadloaf, 2001

They told me to do many things: bleed into your
soup but not too much, genuflect to Freud,
don't use emotional language, pat down the roses
with your bare hands, clip off all their buds,
eat in the dark, don't cook your food,
serve only white things, don't dance, speak
only words of one syllable. They weren't all
wrong. They weren't hostile. They weren't unskilled.
But they weren't useful to me. Except to foster
doubt. Copy this Giacometti drawing,
this painting of Giotto, you will learn,
one said. I will learn to be myself? How
could that be? Make your mountainside
into fortifications, another said, with camouflaged
small robots equipped with tiny pointed objects:
this is not life, you must make it art. Give it darts.
She could be right, who knows, her cactus
self the best guide. Mystery, she said,
mystery is flaccid, a retreat of the
dumb or faint-hearted, where to go only
when you haven't found the point, when
you haven't excavated the spine. Think, she
said, then write what you mean. But then?
What about all the rest? At charades she
was terrible. Words taken from her, she
lost her way, her skills limited to a single
dimension. Her strength and certainty confused me,
confused us all, her strength and her one
powerful book. But I can only be who I am.
All must grow from inside.
They spit. I must spit back. ☉

East Tenth Street

The large Puerto Rican dealer who ran the
block patrolled next to the blue door, the best
grass in the neighborhood. I walked the
south side — less action — waving to
the sax player thru his open window on
the third floor, smiling at his
jazz riffs. The old mattresses laid up against
the Sanitation Department building opposite
my windows leaned forlornly for two days
before the roving truck swept them up. I passed
the tall transvestite in her thick caked makeup
and teased hair, with her umbrella, her
wild eyes. I passed the half-floor-down-from-sidewalk
Chinese laundry and the grumpy Greek guy, small
and sour, who ran the flower stall at
Second Avenue and each spring put up a
hand-lettered sign: "For rent, house on Corfu."
I'd think of the sea and warm quiet as I waited
for the light to change, watching taxis maneuver
past the Second Avenue Deli and St. Mark's
Church where on Tuesdays a green market
cluttered the paved triangle in front
of the gate. One year the crack dealers decided
to be friendly and one would always hold the
unlocked outside door open like a doorman and
say cordially "Good evening!" as I scowled.
But secretly I loved their inventiveness and
the way they made their lives where
no trees grew at all. ❧

Dora Avenue

I'm in the thick of painting beaver ponds,
considering thin silver willow leaves,
while I watch the street for signs of drug
dealing and cops. The neighbors have gotten
cranked up to anger at the new tenants across
the street who behave oddly and drive a noisy
car and have multiple young cats who shit
in all our driveways. Yesterday an old guy
with a brushy grey mustache and an open orange
shirt exposing his chest's dinnerplate-size
tattoo of Jesus squatted by the door behind
the trash bin for an hour. Last night the
house's couple screamed profanities at
each other, and in some obscure
maneuver the cops came and handcuffed
the black-haired woman and took her off.

She'd earlier put a brick through the noisy
car's windshield. Lately I've read pages,
dry and crisp, about altered states of
consciousness: what everyone craves and
needs. Consciousness altered by our
bodies, or with drugs. But what about the
down and dirty real world? And all the while
I think of beavers felling aspen groves,
their razor teeth always growing, so they
need to wear them down or
tear their lips to shreds. ✆

Nora's Dance

The family came in early, Bella riding a
wheel chair, still lively but frail.
Tonight her daughter Nora danced. She'd
made the piece for Bella's slow
departure. She danced with a single spot,
a narrow blade of light spilling
from above, off center, still. In shadow,
moving limb by limb into light, and
out. A quick hand movement or slow, body
spiraling, spiraling. In, then out. Her
white-clad figure nearly blinded. Arc.
Anchor. Spin. Reach and lift and turn,
movement fluid, unexpected, hovering at the
edge of light, the edge of dark, entering,
leaving, held, released. Then nod
goodbye. She walked off downstage left,
from twilight to invisible, slow,
a simple stroll, slow. Abandon, take
leave, bid farewell, exit, a pull like
gravity. She turned only her
head back toward the
dim bare stage,
again and again and again.

Later, Bella's piece from forty years
before: undated, strong, called *Ceremony*:
two powerful men brought in from
L.A. danced, torsos bare and muscled,
and Don, local hero. A sensual feast for
Bella's aging eyes. After the bows, when
the curtain had nearly dropped, but not
quite, the short tawny dancer turned
to pale, pale Don, nearly a foot taller,
reached a hand along his head and
quickly kissed his neck. ⑥

The Last Story of the Night

Long ago, you told me, you abandoned
New Mexico, convinced you should
live again back East. You temporarily
claimed Richmond, in its heart still
a rebel town. Six months later, one
lonely night you thought to sleep
in your sleeping bag, missing something.
Maybe space?
When you pulled it out, you smelled
the lingering scent of smoke.
The trigger. Back West. For good.

Last night was your birthday: a surprise
filled with people I touch paths with
at such things, and see on the river,
gentle unusual folks who, like me,
are aging. We catch up from a year, from
two, I remember what I know of their lives,
remember how it feels to be on a river
with them or others, notice how I feel
no awkwardness, how the simple pleasure
of company balances my time alone,
or with a lover, time more
focused, more important;

but the meal's unbalanced without
such looser company. Or so I feel
this morning, fed by the easy talk
and laughter, the long shared histories
underneath: I have joined the tribe,
barely noticing. And the stories:
like smoke curling through the air,
catching on clothing and hair and
skin, their scents always lingering,
ready to pull us back,
ready, always,
to take us forward. ☙

Section 3

Off
the Map:
Ground
Truth II

Complexity

From fractal dimensions and Fourier transforms,
differential equations and data sets to
ecstatic states, spirit possession, rituals
evoking the six directions and trances.
From quantitative to a distant cave
filled with mammoth bones. Down the hill
from Los Alamos, Santa Clarans dance. Why
is it easier to claim allegiance to
Mandelbrot sets and strange attractors
than to poems? Or poets? Or trances?
Because science works, they claim; it reflects
what's really there, a net of knowledge
that hangs together. Mostly.

Says David Bohm, a physicist with an eye
to explaining everything, where infinite
pilot waves cross are particles, and
that's the implicate order. So what,
say I, clear at least for today I care
about the more robust: rocks and rain and
salt and drumming. A scale within my grasp.
But the *urge* to get at reasons, underpinnings—
now that's the same scale as desire or regret or
even teaching high school history. Some worlds
I don't try to imagine, too involved in the
thoughts of fish or bears or water ouzels,

too enchanted by light shifts across sage
benches, by the air's slide away from
cliffs, squirrels' chatter, a falcon's high
keeee, thunder's shaking threat. They *must*
relate other than through my notice, my
categories, my attentive hours. But how far
down, how far in, how far back, how far
simplified, how far stripped of flesh
to go? Universal Laws, says the famous ecologist,
we must seek Universal Laws. A pleasure of the mind.
But are those laws any real satisfaction?
Are they useful answers? I make another cup of tea.

Eleusis, that ancient place of ritual knowledge had
low mysteries and high mysteries. To reveal
low mysteries brought you punishment. But to
reveal high mysteries? Nothing. High mysteries:
you could not tell them, only do them, only be them.
Description meant no more than a locust's shell:
abandoned, empty, strange. ❧

Life of Stones

Smooth stone, maroon and grey,
fractured in half: a small chip
shows where the hammer struck.
Part holds what once was shell, its
halves still attached, growth rings
visible. Some crystalline glint,
some white deposit at its margin,
then stone grew over shell to its
flat roundness. Shell fossil, but it
could as easily be brain, two halves
clear from the top, mirror images,
but not. Closed, those halves
sheltered soft life, gone before
stonification took off, replacing
molecule with molecule. I wonder
about the seabed there: did
many stones grow like this, each
protecting its coquina, each a
sign that stones and life flow into
each other, a sign that connection
can't be predicted. A soft, pale
mollusc, skilled at filtering
sea water and building an elegant
smooth shell in some distant sea
began a trail that led, finally, to this
maple table where a round tin of
Badger lip balm, almost its exact size,
keeps the split stone company.

Finally?
No. Not finally. But here and
now, hinged between time's
two halves where molecule
overtakes molecule overtakes
molecule.
Always. ☺

Pumping Ions

Our nerves excite each other
with the tiniest change of charge
across their membranes:
inside to outside. Ions of sodium,
potassium, calcium zoom back and forth.
Chloride, in its negative state
usually hangs outside. The
difference, positive to negative,
whips along the axons, a wave of
charge. Then at the tiny gap
between one neuron and another
molecular messengers swim the
chasm, send on the pulse, and
dissolve, or swim back with a butterfly kick
or backstroke. And their slight malfunction—
too much, too little—can make us crazy: manic,
psychotic, depressed. More astonishing yet,
molecular receivers, like docking ports more
particular than Yale locks mated to their keys,

also match molecules from poppies or from coca
leaves; and our minds quirk up, or
calm down, or lose their moorings
altogether. Can there be any firmer proof
the world and our minds share their
alphabets, their ways of moving,
their mysteries? ☙

Altered States

For days I read and read, then struggled
with the pieces, trying to jigsaw them
together to make my own picture. I had it
in mind: the way we live in a repeating
cycle of wake, sleep, dream, wake, sleep, dream,
counting on our prayer wheels as we circle the
stupa built of painted stones, old wood,
brass bells. And as we circle, the moving
ostinato under all our melodies
from birth picks up trouble, automatic
stumbling steps, disturbances we can't avoid,
blank spots we can't see. Our world
narrows, our melodies lose their open
endedness: we are not at fault, it always
happens that way, repeating cycles comforting
but deadly. But, like Jung's claim a trio
always needs a fourth, another way of mind
can shake the ostinato beat, allow us to be
more ourselves, alive to who we are, the
thorns pulled from our feet so we can stop
that old limp, dance our melodies—we think
and feel and sing and love at once, the
ostinato broken into tabla rhythms. It is
a flash, a flash of consciousness out of
daily rounds, but no less belonging to our
bodies, belonging to our selves.

We can't stay there long, but we can bring it
back with us. I found the words two days ago
and as they snapped in place, their meanings
expanded, my body knew what I'd said was
right, but until that moment, the fragments
ruled, the engine wouldn't catch, the music
didn't swing. And then it did. ✆

Poems Are Like Dreams

Dreams gather particulars.
They come of their own accord: the
dog who barks or the elevator which
never comes, the vision of your grandmother's
crocheting, her crossword puzzles, her
made-from-scratch birthday cakes with icing
as sweet as plain honey. And those
signs brought forth circle around each
other so the song they sing calls up
loss, or fear of failure, or
desire, or power beyond your waking
life: levitate and fly above the streets,
the hills, the snow-laden clouds,
threading through eddies of air, swimming
as if you were in water clear and light and
breathable, released from leaden
gravity, though keeping stable requires
some pull, some tether of force to
stroke against. But the feelings can
be played out in multiple ways, your back
leg twitching as you chase the rabbit
in your sleep, try to catch what you've
never reached, or only held a moment
at a time. Your neurons spark, your
neuro-peptides circulate like
hurricanes, you write it down. ✆

Tidal Pull

The easily comprehensible only offers
temporary relief. The old categories
cushion you for awhile, before you sink back
into known comfort—this has worked
for many, why not for me? Why resist
any longer? Take it, it's given, you've
been blind, it's here—some wisdom you can
trust as you trust the sun will rise each
morning, even through dense clouds. You
trust it, whatever it is does its job
for awhile, lighting your sparks,
expanding, expanding—until the pieces
of the puzzle which didn't fit before
begin to reappear. The engine's all together
and you have a handful of bolts left over.
Or worse, you've put the engine back together
and it's no longer what runs your VW, but
an elephant trumpeting on the beach. And
you're left without any motor at all. Ride
the elephant? Oh yes. Of course. Mythic
underpinnings, archetypes chasing each
other through the pines, deep releases, images
from nowhere, pleasures without explanation.
But after awhile they too recede at a run,
like tides in the Bay of Fundy, docks left so
high above damp rocks they seem like
observation towers. Then what? Wait for
the next tide? Know nothing? Despair of
ever knowing more? Despair of any relief
longer than a moon cycle, longer than a
flash of spirit? Is there any answer between
the mundane and unknowable rest? ๑

Why Ask for More?

Why ask for more?
Why want to know how things work?
Why worry about the brain? Consciousness?
Why pile up facts and processes
like a pack rat collects pop-top tabs,
cholla skeletons, and lost tissues, cementing
them all together with sticky pee?
Why do that?
Why wonder?
Why hope to rearrange it all so it
makes sense?
Why think making sense will
make a difference?
The dog barks at some imagined badger,
because he needs something to do.
Do I make the same noisy feints?
No. Slowly, always, the world clarifies,
meanings materialize like clouds, become
carved soapstone, slide into
my pocket and I look around
for more. I ask for more because
it feeds me, no less than toasted bagels
or ripe peaches or salsa
and chips. My neurons chomp down
on thoughts, on words, on stories, chewing
with electrical teeth, swallowing with
their impossibly complicated networks,
metabolizing words and movement
and relationships and light. Without
that, I would starve. ◐

Fine Distinctions

Hokey, I ask—what exactly
makes *spiritual* hokey or OK?
I don't know except
it's like good art or bad art.
Plastic santos from New Jersey,
Jesus calendars, *soul retrieval*,
animal helpers, St. Christopher medals,
the Virgin of Guadalupe painted on a
low rider's side, the discarded
crown of thorns beside the Medanales
church after Easter week, kosharis
painted in black and white stripes,
Jerry Falwell on TV, radio rantings
from the Bible, posting the Ten Commandments
in schools, missionaries, channeling Seth,
calling to the four directions, swinging incense,
blessing animals in St. John the Divine,
arranging stones in a circle, chanting,
giving up beer during Lent, being celibate,
fasting in the wild, eating peyote,
hot dish suppers in the church basement,
Styrofoam ornaments for the plastic
Xmas tree, E. Power Biggs, a naming
dance from Mali, a pilgrimage to
the sea, in white, to honor Yemaya?
Where are the lines? ۞

A dove coos under less mellow
birds, the cane rattles,
traffic rumbles on the
freeway, a plane crosses overhead, my neighbor's
screen door opens and closes, invisible on the
other side of the wood fence covered with
honeysuckle, a grackle sends out one piercing
screech, far down the block a dog barks, but
not for long, another barks
closer, and my back neighbor's sprinklers
kick in, first sputtering then easing into a
constant hiss. No one mowing lawns, no
mega bass driving down the street, no
hammering, no distant sound of TV voices,
that particular annoying rhythm, no sirens,
no garbage truck growls, no cats yowling.
No sound of surf, no rattling vent covers,
no music from my machines, no radio
voices. A sudden flock of sparrows descends
on the ripe cherries. And what of the voices
in my head? Do they require cataloging?
The voices, and the sounds of flutes, steel
drum orchestras, cello melodies, string quartets,
African drums. Water trickling over stones
in the desert. A spring flowing from the
bottom of a sandstone wall. Hummingbird
buzz. Silence. ☙

In the Trees

I'll hang bells in the trees—
in the apricot, the nectarine,
the piñon—
and in the wind they'll
ring their high notes and startle
grackles off, purely functional—
bells in the trees
tinking and chiming
like noisy prayer flags or
the elfin forest garden on the
coast of Maine, or the
piñon over the Stone Lions Shrine
hung with feathers for prayers.
Trees, dressed for dancing, given an
extra voice, percussion
metallic and sweet.
I will wear bells on my ankles
bells on my neck, bells on my wrists
and the wind will blow me like
a coyote willow, a Lombardy poplar, like
green palm fronds, and I'll jingle
and clank and quietly peel, and
rattle and vibrate, loud and warming,
raucous and impossible to miss. ⊚

Hippocampus: Greek for Seahorse

The hippocampus, curved and slightly fluted,
is divided left and right, lapped around
each temporal lobe in our brains,
deep inside.

The seahorse floats
upright, clinging to seaweed with
her tapering coiled tail.

The hippocampus moves not at all,
but the way its neurons fire,
the way their fingers reach outward
makes us sad or ecstatic, eager or
depressed.

The male seahorse incubates his
young in his ventral pouch, kangaroo-like.

Hippocampus halves, when throbbing slowly with
electric beats in synch, put us in
trance, bring on transcendent certainty.
Some crucial cells have died, perhaps,
leaving us unable to compare
contradictions so we leap over
all paradox with joy.

The seahorse suspended in seagrass
flutters her delicate lateral
fins, fan-shaped, and feels the
tide turn, salty sea pulled into
treacherous currents once again,
pulled and pulled,
pulled always by
the ever-circling moon.
She remains suspended, the sea grass
on the move, responsive, the sea grass
angled with the tide,
anchors holding fast. ☙

Section 4

Invocations

(Athena, Hermes, Aphrodite)

Invocation: Athena

Round river stone, polished by water,
darker than moon, but moon grey. Not perfect,
but almost perfect, fitting exactly into
palm, cool, heavy. Circle made not
by radius and diameter, but by rock
tumbling past time. Grey-eyed Athena.
Mind, but more than mind:
wisdom, even power—
for the hundredth time,
thank you.

Memory: echoing marble halls, vast, impressive,
the National Gallery, a monument to thought. Cool
round room with fountain in its center, light
filtering down from a circular window high above.
Chill in the swamp heat of DC's summer, echoing
with footsteps and fountain splash. Dark
marble, green and shadowy, shot through with white,
blue, grey, a few veins of rust, milled to wide
columns like tree trunks supporting the distant vault.
And art: a frozen nymph, a frozen face, passageways
spoking outward from the shiny floor to pale busts of
Caesars, angular Cezannes, glittering altarpieces
from Byzantium, dark Rembrandts. The booty of history,
the booty of time for making culture. But I went there
because it was quiet and cool, mystical and musical—
a grove made to resemble this one where I sit—
though no one knew it, not even me.

Here: ochre sand, pale rocks, spare stream plants
growing among ponderosa needles, baked by sun, smelling
like all ponderosa forests along these valleys, sweet and
dense. This sandstone isn't smooth like Athena's
stone, but angular, cracked, gravel roughened; still,
the small stream sings, the breeze lets the grasses
dance, the shadows sway in place. Is this mind?
Is this wisdom?
The cool circular stone rests beside this
flowing stream, broken trunks grey along its banks,
quick butterfly bright orange,
rush of wind. ◉

Invocation: Hermes

Quicksilver. I hold a tiny vial, its mercury bouncing,
splitting, reconnecting. Heavy in hand and
quivering, bright as silver, bright as
moon, but fluid. And poisonous in
the wrong places—in fish bodies, for example,
a toxic substance. Hermes, you're neither silver
nor toxic, but invisible and palpable in this
water beside me, in the fountain in the National
Gallery's marble hall, a Mercury bronzed in winged
sandals, winged hat—narrow contrivances meant
to catch your wiliness and motion. Guide me.
You're never clear, you never fail to make a leap.
Open me to energies that liven the wind, these
dancing green stalks, these water striders riding
the interface of air and water, at home only
where the two meet. Now you see them, now they're
gone, their shadows sliding over the pool's sand
bottom. Water, light, sun, night. The underworld,

the overworld, the worlds unseen, your strange precise
guidance. In league with Athena. In league with
Aphrodite. In league with my own heart. Otherwise
how could you work so well? You're the one
I need most, need to trust, need to help me
understand I need not look back. Carry me
on your sandals—or loan them to me for
awhile. Give me, please, the ease of your
words, your certainty in guidance. Keep me
clear about what I'm doing, but not so clear
I'm rigid. Loose. Quicksilver and fleet. Practical
and completely gratuitous, like the color of this
butterfly, the perfect gifts from nowhere.
Bless me. Bless us all. ☉

Invocation: Aphrodite

You're such a friend. This stream may be more
yours than Athena's, a warrior dressed for
battle no matter how wise. I've brought this
bone for you, to be your emblem. A flat s-curve,
one end more curved than the other, split to
its two joint pieces, white and flaking off
in layers, two labels tied to the thinner, more
curved end, for everyone who can't recognize it:
"Texas toothpick," "raccoon penis bone."
Those raccoons. Who would know their cocks are
stiffened with bone from looking at their curious
blackened eyes, their grey bushy backs disappearing
over garbage cans and away? The idea
of a penis bone tickles me. The phallic
certainty. But Aphrodite, that *is* part of
what you're about: fucking, penis hard enough
to thrust into vagina, smooth and soft and
gooey. But you're about much more: the light
touch of hand on back, gentle, not sexual.
You're about taking on another's phrasing, tone
of voice, wandering mind, uncertainties and
awkwardnesses. You're about exchanging
sensation: part sexual, mostly sensual, deep
opening, answers only bodies can give, conversations
of nerve and muscle. Aphrodite, you've blessed me
royally, and I am grateful beyond measure. But
you are trying me now and your laughter rings
like the melodious riffles next to me. You're
in league with Hermes and have some agenda, but
it escapes me. Give me peace or give me pleasure,

some release, though I know release only lasts
an hour, a day. You just complicate everything,
it's been said—but 'tain't true; you put
the life in it all. Of all raccoon love, only this
5-inch bone lies curved in my hand; but of all my
love, what remains is the flavor of my life, the
fastness of binding, the freedom of sex, the
certainty of self.
Ah, Aphrodite, I wouldn't have it any other
way. You've changed my life many times, you're
changing it again, and only an oracle
could tell how. But no matter.
I trust you. ✆

Section 5

Ecologies of the Heart: Open Systems

Comparative Anatomy

Male. Female. In that Duke lab
long ago with formaldehyde zapping
our brain cells we dissected our
cats, one cat per person. We each had
the same lungs and stomachs, the same
kidneys and livers, but when we got
to the *reproductive system*, we split into
two factions and needed to share. Vas
defferens, fallopian tubes, prostate, cervix,
uterus, testicle. We were twenty, or nineteen,
sailing into our lives, fearless one
day, terrified the next. We poked with
our scalpels, laughed and joked,
swallowed our unease. I was as
tough as the guys, as unembarrassed,
as filled with my capacity to learn
facts, to grasp how things worked. I had
a crush on the lab instructor, older
and large-boned, probably all of twenty-four.
One week my male table mates teased
one good old boy, from
Greensboro or Tarboro, who took it half
sheepishly, half proudly, "Yup, she just
breezed in and snarfed him up. He never
knew what hit him!" I pointed out
seminal vesicle, ejaculatory duct;
my partner, careful with his probe,
pointed out ovary, follicle, and then,
relieved, we moved on to our separate
feline brains with their pale, spongy
tissues and tough white nerves. ✿

The Model

Driven by desire?
Pan-sexual, pan-amorous,
pan-erotic? The world pulling
me, reeling in my tether, reeling
out my kite string. Is it the same
as the itch of sex? The hollowness
that reverberates with silent ringing
echoes inside my sacrum. A friend once
said, "When I want it, I want it NOW."
and *now* finds herself content with sex
but too home-bound, missing diving,
the wet, the salt, the sun.
Is it gender, is it fear, is it sadness
that's the difference? Was it not always
the best, but not the all, for me —
my inner alloys magnetized to it,
others magnetized to me because —
because why? I liked it, I liked them,
regardless of all else? The luck of my
hormone balance, my grateful happiness
to lose control, to give and receive
at once, the attention total, both
directions. It was never an orgasm quest —
they came too easy, too often for me to notice
any temporary lack. But still, it was the
best I had then,
the model for everything, everything. ⚭

Morning, June

Li, said a friend, is Chinese for the
easy pattern of grain in wood.
This table's maple veneer answers,
its patterns bow and swell, crowd
each other and spread out. Or perhaps
li is the line, only, of a larger
pattern; as easy, but less inclusive.
Unfocused disks of light spot
the table with bright medallions, move
and vibrate as breeze sways cane
outside the window. Another friend once
asked, her German never fully
translated, "What is *dappled*?"

We all aim for *li*, I think. But
perhaps I am presumptuous, perhaps
I must claim that only for myself.
Or perhaps *li* is a concept that sounds
useful, but draws its power
from opposition: to force, say,
or straight, or parallel, or
tightly regulated. But if grain
in wood is *li*, what is dappled
morning sun dancing across my table,
over wood and notebook, pens and
erasers, over my moose cup and the
round rock, grey and flat, crossed
with a pale red line, tumbled in some
distant stream to the smoothness of
shoulder skin? ❧

Puzzle Boxes

I had half a dozen:
their inlaid wood designs
hid sliding panels which revealed
latches; or whole sides would shift.
The first puzzle boxes must have
kept many secrets. I kept nothing in mine.
The value of those small containers
smelling of sandalwood
was not what they held but
the elegance of their entry. Manipulate
all their pieces in exactly the right
order and the inner chamber opens. The box
meant more than its contents: it meant
the mind behind its idea, the hands
skillfully fashioning it. I admired
the inventiveness, the craft. But more,
the box was what I wished to be then—
nicely put together, though at first glance
inaccessible beyond my surface.
But if you knew the tricks, had a light
enough touch, paid attention, the plain
inner room would open with
a smooth, easy,
surprising release. ⚇

Durham, 1969

She watched the wind
from the bathroom window,
wrapped in a blanket
in the middle of the night,
Durham's leaves
by early May full-grown,
tumbling in anchored waves.
From that house full of
unexpected bedmates, the
famous poet appeared
also unable to sleep, stood
with her watching the
blowing night, wrapped in
his own blanket. We've
had our troubles, he said of
his wife, in Madison or St. Paul,
but we've finally worked it out.
The wine and bourbon of the
post-reading parties beginning
to wear off, the stamp of academic
approval fading into lives
rearranging themselves, poet-
catalyzed, wind-carried.
I wasn't there, but I know.
I've watched the wind.
I know. ☙

Oregon Inlet

A front moved through last night,
just after dark, rattling vent covers
on the roof, sending loose plastic bags
into the apricot's branches, its buds
ready to pop any day. From our single fixed
points, always sudden weather.

Long ago, at Oregon Inlet, you and I trudged
far out on the bank where waves
broke in wild foaming cordons. We were
upset: I'd told you I'd slept with your
best friend, my best friend.
Your hurt and anger surpassed
anything I'd imagined. We were airing
out by moving through openness, at the
edge of rolling ocean. We knew the
storm threatened: it's hard to miss
weather on the Outer Banks where no hill
taller than a sleeping dog blocks the
sky. But when the fury hit it nearly knocked
us over. We faced the gale to struggle
home—we had no choice—the rain and
sand stung us, blown by pewter winds. We
leaned into it like cartoons. You said,
"We weren't too smart to come out here,"
as we fought against the storm, nearly
blinded, soaked, released then from our
own swirling distress, tied to each other
by our tiny humanness in the vastness of the
raging, faultless elements. ❧

You sat across from me under the shady
arbor, the wind threatening to blow our
sandwich baskets off the small
table as we lingered alone through the
afternoon. You had become thin,
your blue eyes larger than ever under
bushy brows; your ears had become
prominent and pointed, as if they'd
stayed in place while your skull had
retreated; I remembered them differently.
You were stooped from hours, years in front
of your computer at the Press. You loved your
son—a child who might have been mine
once, but wasn't—and feared you would
die soon. I spoke from my heart, from who
I had become, yet felt beside me the one
I had been when I knew your body
well, shared your meals and dreams. She—
the one gone forever—threatened to impose
her language, her rhythms, her
uncertainties, her elliptical equivocations,
her learned responses to you—but didn't.

Couldn't. What had I expected? Had I expected
anything? You were not the one I had
loved. Time had changed us both almost
beyond recognition. You were funny and kind
and mostly easy with your dissolved dreams.
Your old self flashed through.
As we hugged goodbye I felt your bones
so fragile, so fragile. ☉

She stood in the crowded xerox shop,
waiting with her pile of art: sea turtles.
A man, tan and blond,
leaned over her right arm and said
after he'd looked at the top page
a moment, "Green turtle?" Yes. But how
would someone in downtown New York
know that? They talked while they waited.
"I'm an undersea photographer," he said.
Oh yeah? she thought. He told her his name
and she looked at him harder, seeing
his images of chambered nautiluses, south
Pacific reefs, filtered light in coffee table
books: no one with a camera in the ocean
had a better eye. "Would you like to come up
to my room? I live upstairs," he said as
she paid for her copies. Upstairs on 8th Street
in Manhattan? In a residence hotel, a little
sleazy for such a name, such a reputation.
The room was nearly solid with stained
pine furniture encircling a double bed. He put
Scarlatti (or was it Scriabin?) on his
high-end music machines and assumed
she'd come upstairs for sex. Had she?

She didn't know, but she didn't have her
diaphragm, and they nipped and licked
each other instead. And in those
hours and the week after, she learned he
not only lived to dive, he lived always
under a sea where mania alternated with
depression. He gave her a set of page proofs:
sea lions curled around each other, playing,
one nipping another's shoulder, their wet fur
dark and shining. ✿

Rehoboth Beach

A pier in the distance,
jutting into dark ocean,
covered with rides and lights,
everyone slightly burned from
the day's lounge on the beach, hot
sand, Coppertone smell, cold waves,
creosote under boardwalk, cigarette
butts half in sand at bottom of pilings.
Showers concrete, sandy, damp, echoing
with voices. At night still hot, boardwalk
crowded and bright. John and Ernie and
another guy yelling "Delay!" on the rides.
I'm mystified until Sandy takes me
aside and explains it's a product that
delays men's ejaculations. We're all virgins,
13, 14. She's embarrassed, I still barely
understand and don't get why it's an issue
or why it's funny.

I love the rides that turn my stomach most,
that spin me and make the bottom drop away,
no hint of nausea, unease, just wild
sensation. We walk against the streaming
crowd awhile, intent on being non-conformists,
then I drag them all to the other side, where
we walk the same direction as everyone else —
I say, "It's too easy to not conform by walking
on the left, it's a cop out. We have to walk
the same direction, but really be different,
not just on the surface." Sandy has no idea
what I'm talking about; John, years later, will
sadly nurse an unrequited passion for me, and
I will only wish he'd go away. &

First Love

She's twenty-two, in love for the first time,
two months past her first fuck,
as distracted as if she were swarmed
by black flies. Except no biting, only
a longing for his company, his touch,
her body answering, craving the feeling
of a nest, of becoming herself
without the distancing of intellect,
of finally coming home to a family who
will always be there. Or so it feels in her
flushed love. I remember my own relief
and astonishment, how I expanded in a
week to fill the shape that had been
waiting for me. But her lover's Guatemalan,
likes her, but also likes men, and
without a doubt likes the idea of finding
himself in the States: she's an angel
of escape. After the escape, will
she cease wearing wings? After the
escape, will he stop feeling like home to her and
become a bitter taste, dark and needy,
impossible to rinse away? I know
the feel of the life before—

hungry, uncertain, wanting—and the life
after—temporarily filled, doubt-free,
where wanting stops aching because
you are answered, over and over and over and you
can't imagine anything will ever stop those
warm answers. But she's twenty-two, still fresh
in the wider world, unaware of how
much more waits past this first wild opening.
And perhaps she has yet to develop the simple
habit of trusting her own life. ✆

Monsters I

Has anyone seen the monsters
lately, the ones who thread your spine
through the furnace or the ones who eat you
and eat you and eat you?

Haven't you wanted always to burn,
to learn how to light the match then
not be consumed?
The monsters are within.
They eat you from the inside.
But let them out and they become
your playmates, not evil,
not sucking out your life, but
plotting with you, thinking up
escapades, part of your gang
of one. Your gang of many
monsters. But wait, who calls them
monsters? I think they might be friends.
Why mince around? They *are* friends.

The dictionary says of monsters:
one who deviates from normal behavior
and
a threatening force
and
one who is highly successful
and
more at MIND.
The monsters. Ah. Let's go find them.
We'll let them out and play. ✿

Monsters II

Thanks Demons, for chewing at my stomach
when my heart's thrown back in my face;
thanks for nipping at my heels, holding
my elbows to remind me of all the times
I've turned away from steep stairs, from
a fog too dense; thanks Demons for
disguising yourselves as escape routes,
for greasing the way. But I'm not grateful
for the sleep you've required of me, the
solitude mixed with longing.
And I'm not wholly behind my gratitude.
I'd rather thank the sun, space, the
mountains, the ones I love, the ones who
love me, now and in the past; the world's
complexity and beauty, its calm
implacability, where Demons don't exist.
In the cloisters' paintings, contorted faces
on the flying monsters are faces of small,
furry bats: dark for night, ridged in dense
swirling patterns so the insect nabbers
can understand their world of echoes.
So they can live. So much for monsters.
The faces of my Demons? If I see them
clearly and understand, will
they cease tangling in my hair and
go back to ricocheting from one bug to
another in the darkness behind my
eyes? The Demons come in waves,
screeching and squeaking, but they intend
no mischief: they simply live
their lives the way they can. ❧

Can We Eat Together?

The only two great subjects,
someone said, are food and sex.
I'll share my lentils, lemons, linguine,
olives if you'll include me
in your pesto, peaches, persimmons,
and pistachioed pieces of baklava.
Of questionable motives: besides
the steaming soup and swallows
of iced pears in chocolate, I mean
to follow back your words along
their fleshy trails: the nut crunch,
expressoed, buttered scones that built
the furniture of your self, on past
the present future fires, metabolisms
leveling gorgonzola to a hot equivalent
of shrimp and of the latest
just-discovered Sappho fragments.
It only matters, it always matters,
how the flavors mix and blend
how the flavors mix and grow. ☉

Long Afternoon

We sat on the patio, both striped by the shade
of cane stalks overhead, eating slowly on the
plate of fruit: yellow mango, green melon,
sweet strawberries; I listened to you
talk about returning to healthy alignment:
of head, of *hara*, and of the heart, a delicate node
less centered than open, or perhaps closed down,
protecting its seed. And more. About movement
and how we are the only living beings not
obligatorily aligned. That accounts for
the pull we feel from nature. And more.
We finished the fruit and retreated to the
cool house where first we followed your
recent days on road maps, then stretched parallel
on the bed, aligned horizontally with
ourselves and each other, understanding
but not understanding, passing a new gate,
but a gate we'd passed many times, always
knowing the garden would somehow be changing
as we entered it again. ✤

Klein Blue

Yesterday I painted the chair Klein blue:
blue shaded violet, darker than
cornflowers, lighter than dusk sky.
That blue means one thing in the art
world; here it protects from the evil eye.
Paint doors blue, paint gates blue, paint
window frames blue to keep the house safe.
Not something to say, but something
to see, to sit in, to feel hard under my buns,
to protect me from myself, as I sit in the
patio, shuffling words and memories. He left
yesterday. For three weeks. But that's
not why I painted the chair blue to
match the lobelia. His leaving has left me
more alone for now; but those minor demons of
solitude threaten less than the demons
of the stuck record, the tape loop, the same
song on the juke box, the same meal every
day. And yet. The repetition matters less than
the incompleteness. The incompleteness
requires the reprise, until finally I can turn
the last corner so the next round will
be different. The paint dried overnight.
Yesterday the chair was red. Today it's
Klein blue. ◉

The Dream

Encumberance: demanding much attention,
returning little for the effort. Tenacious,
persistent, yelling in my ears. A white
elephant, an albatross—something which
no longer serves. But is this understanding
based on economic theory? Give attention,
give energy, give food and drink, give warmth
and a bed of straw. Then you should expect
a return to match what you've given. It's a
barter, where what you get must match
what you give or it's a bad deal, not wise,
inefficient and not functional. Dumb. Informed
by the wind or subterranean rumblings, not
good sense. But love is not a barter. A gift
cannot be a barter, or it ceases being gift.
Can the answer be to love the white elephant?
Giving her water to spray over her back is
an easy task: not an investment. Love. The
albatross, after all, still flies on long thin
wings, gliding over the seas. You have not
killed her, she doesn't hang heavy and
bleeding around your neck, feathers askew.
Let go what no longer serves you: the repeated
suggestion, the repeated hope. Perhaps first
you must feed it, give it provisions and a
map, then it will feel safe to go off into
the world without you. Or, like the white
elephants at the sea's edge, roll in surf
and dissolve, limb by limb, into
foaming, roaring breakers. ☙

You Said

You said, "He put wind in your sails,"
with no overlays of jealousy. You knew
you'd been wind before, were still;
I knew you'd partly given me the sails,
gaff-rigged my boat, sailed with me. But
you were right: not that I'd been
becalmed, in a back water, stymied, but
I had felt the jib and mainsail fill and
strain against their lines unexpectedly,
white canvas blowing out and glittering
in the sun, pulling against mast, against
blocks as lines played out and bow cut
waves, splashing salt water into damp air.
Trim the jib, we're heeled over, with
a direction in mind if not a destination,
dependent on the breeze, its strength
variable, uncertain, no storms backing
wind around. Tack east, zigzag on the
chart, calipers ready, pacing off distances
over buoyant sea, watching for shoals,

buoys, listening for bells and horns. But
it's my boat, the wind simply what's
given me a driving impulse, a sudden
but sustained energy to sail on, to
speed—where? Neither forward
nor back nor to the distant light house.
Simply to sail, to swell with invisible
energy. I head the boat thus, let out the
mainsheet and capture the breath of the
breathing all around me, of *your* uncertain,
of *your* sure, of *your*
unbounded gusty weather. ◉

Sex is Informative

Sex is informative.
Or so I've just claimed elsewhere
trying to tweak experience
into logic, or explanation, or
thinly veiled self-promotion.
What hasn't someone thought of,
said smoothly or awkwardly
or with elaborate filigrees?
But this week isn't last week,
despite the familiar markers;
the skin reacts with new
leaps, new melting slides
and what might once have
been a roller coaster dip and
quick curve has become
a sail at dawn in a gaff-rigged
wooden boat along a mangrove
coast, spoonbills and night herons
peering out at incoming tide.
What might have told me
how to shift my weight to keep
my wind-surfer up to speed
now suggests your heart's fractal
branchings, the canyons in your
memory's watershed ripe with
early spring, my answering rivers,
banks willow-full and fragrant. ❧

Section 6

Ecologies of the Heart: Cycle I

Somerset Reservoir

Sun sear on black ice crossed with cracks,
perforated with bubbles, pearls
unstrung. We slide down tilted ice skin
and penguin walk from snow island to
snow island, ice giving back washed blue,
white, sienna, grey trees. We keep twenty feet
apart, necessity a mirror of our unease
together. We stop. A mink runs in
flex-backed awkwardness between us and
the sun: movement, dark and silhouetted
in the pale arena, a shadowed liveliness.
We find her tracks: small with signs of
dragging tail. Past the ice-locked hummock
we stop again and turn our heads to
listen to the low, reverberating gurgles
blossoming into cold air just off shore—a low
booming we can't explain, but spend hours
discussing as we traverse the cracking, moaning
ice, more alive, more strangely alive than the
forest creeks still trickling between frozen banks.
A drumhead of ice, stretched seven miles? Or
only the disjunct between ice and water, separated
by airy space—only a little distance clips the
hard connection and lets the solid winter world
speak to us in tongues of brittleness, in percussive
tongues, where words have been restored to their
minimal requirement: liquid against air in
an echoing chamber. We walk among muttering
ice beings, we hear ice secrets, but between our own
warm bodies pass no secrets at all, our mouths frozen,
uncertain, far from any thaw. ☙

Vermont

These hills swell and breathe, threaded
together by twisting roads, trails through
stripped trees and sodden leaves. A lone figure
crosses the field from the studio and
enters the forest, heading downhill. The
roads wind in a mysterious order I can't
know or even begin to grasp, my
orientation skills here no better than
a balloon aloft, a feather adrift.
The town of Victorian buildings furnishes
the local locus, quiet and gently busy,
like the half-frozen creeks that drain these
hillsides, slowly flowing over rocks, through
pools, by the skeleton sweat lodge, its
saplings bound together with cord, by the grey
slate ring around fire gravel. The town pools
cars and fires of woodstoves, the bookstore
run by a man who once lived south of Santa Fe,
its shelves graced by *Coyote's Canyon*, Andy
Goldsworthy's rocks and leaves and ice crystals,
compass points for my disorientation. The
heavy skies shield the sun, even the shadows
blocked from pointing west or east;
and dusk leans into the roads as we
drive back through the quiet labyrinth,
white, narrow birches lighting the
roadsides like solid beacons,
pointing straight up
to the sky. ☺

Sinking In

And we sank into language, finally,
like sinking into a warm sea, the ice dissolved,
gone as if it never had held the water
at bay. The surface closed over our
heads and we grew gills and
fins and our bodies began to flex in
tune with the swells and because we were
entrained with the rolling sea, the waves
of words, finally we meshed with each other,
and what we knew, however tentative
and provisional, found its way across the
gulf between us, across the bubbling
liquid language to infiltrate the
spaces between our shirts and skins,
between our skins and pulsing blood.
Words. One next to another, in strings, lines
through time, but they always
looped back and back and back then forward,
dissolving into ourselves more completely the
closer they matched our inner understandings,
until no distance at all remained. We sank,
breathing a primal unbound substance,
melodic and charged, and for hours we swam
unburdened by our lives, past or future,
finding our momentary selves enough—

enough though we worked at making sense,
we worked at getting at some claim on
what is real, not minding that the answers
eluded us, not minding that we'd temporarily
lost our will to find the surface.
The real surrounded us, held us
gently, and the breathing sea swept us
imperceptibly through the light into
an embracing
illuminated
dark. ☙

Coiled Serpents

My life is mine; yours is yours.
But to keep track, suddenly, of where
you are and when, the Yucatan,
Vermont, Death Valley, adds a layer
to my wandering mind, what I
inscribe on my inner calendar, its
rock spirals suddenly reconfigured
into snakes and frogs and laughing
lizards, all fluid creatures
whose blood responds to sun, whose
liveliness depends on warmth and
flowing blood and whose clocks are
tuned to daily rhythms in a way
ours aren't. My clock's tuned these
days to a constant wash of words,
the sea, at depth, where light
rarely reaches. I tumble until
I'm thrust upward into light again,
but never to the surface. I
sink again, unsure how deep
I've gone, with no way to predict
how long I'll be there. But somewhere,
in my pancreas, my liver, perhaps even in
my heart I know you're out in air,
your calendar coiling and uncoiling
like rock serpents dance when we've
finally turned our backs and moved
on down the trail, the wind singing,
the wind singing,
the wind always singing. ☙

Iguanas

The iguanas sun themselves, green
and scaley, eating crunchy beetles,
wiggly ants, but mostly barely mobile
in tropical heat. At 5th Avenue and
13th Street the huge iguana on the roof
kept getting stolen. One day there, twenty
feet of painted lizard staring down on
traffic, the next, a bare roof. In
Key West, the iguana man always comes to
the pier for sunset, brown and wrinkled,
riding his bike, an iguana or two
lounging on his shoulders under
frayed brim. The iguanas sun themselves
in the Yucatan, next to Mayan ruins,
next to tourist bars, small dragons
with mysterious minds. I have no
grounding here, only imagination,
remembered humid heat, remembered
sea, remembered iguanas, remembered
tourist bars, remembered *pictures*
of Mayan ruins. But it is not iguanas
that interest me here, it is their
sunning, their languid stillness,
their geographic coordinates which
place one, many, near your warm,
toasting skin. ☙

Spence Hot Spring

Up the other side of the canyon the hot pool
steamed. We sat at first in the car,
pelted with wet snow, and talked of *containers*
to increase the heat in groups, in couples,
the exits closed, the lid on, the steam
cooking, healing psychic wounds. I talked of time
as a container. You talked of agreed-upon rules: no
fantasies of other lovers, say. The
snow stopped, we negotiated muddy paths
downhill, across a lively stream, up among
roots to a stone enclosure: four naked men sat
quietly neck deep in hot water. We stripped
and stepped in, to cook gently under close
clouds, under ponderosas smelling of pitch
and wind. In time the pool's population changed:
an air force guy about to move to Iceland
where their thermal springs heat
greenhouses large enough to support banana
plantations, and six college kids from Minnesota
on spring break. The light slowly faded to
a dim softness, the drizzle misted over us, our
bodies eased. We dressed and headed
down in gathering shadows, trying not to slip
in wet, well-worn braided trails. You
asked, "Number 4?" referring to my list, postponed as
we'd left the car. On my list, #4 read, *contradictory
impulses, internal release*. I kept my silence
until we'd driven some miles back down the
road, then restarted our exchange of words,

as we watched the wet night through
windshield unmarked by flying sand. The heater
blew it free of any vapors, our moist breaths
mingling in the swirling air
contained between us. ◎

Autonomy

It's what Tibet wants from
China. You are not a country, but
autonomy's what you've fought so
hard to gain. You've never
been a colony, a protectorate, a
conquered land, though that's how
you've felt: dependent, needy, a slave
to another's whims, taxes exacted from
your emotional lands in order that
you could survive. Autonomy—it's
what I've always had: independence,
self-determination, trade between
free nations, the authority to make
foreign policy on my own, fly my own
flag, speak my own language, eat
my own foods, make my own laws.
Not pay tribute to another. You
claim to have regained your
sovereignty, so you can finally make
your own treaties, pursue your
national interests outside your borders
because you've discovered gold, you've
hit oil, you've invented a product the world
will pay for. But you still have your
history inscribed on the inside of your
skin, and your foreign office isn't
quite sure of itself, your Air Force constantly
flying sorties along your coast, your Navy
at full alert. I saw you as someone free
to enter into treaties, into trade agreements,
free to call off the Border Guards. But I'd not
known what a young country you really were. ◈

Is He Like the Peacock?

Is he like the peacock, his visionary
feathers spread in two-dimensional
display? Real, but not quite what he seems,
though exactly what he is? Or like the
hummingbird whose freefalls and
quick pull ups a second before the
ground join with a descending
Morse code siren, high and eerie, an
emissary from another world in
desert dusk? Or is he like the invisible
blue grouse in dense thickets along the
foothills of the Rockies, calling like a
movie monkey with rising, panting
hoots? Displays for love, temporary
and deluding? Or does it depend on who
reads the cues? Or whether they
mean the same to actor and to audience?
We're human, not mating birds, and
how we signal gives many meanings.
But I'm surprised at how
his plumes and knowing eyes sprout
from such a small, warm animal curled
around itself in a cold room on a wind-swept
plain. I've known he wasn't putting on a show
for me, or for any other woman; I've known no
one is quite what their costumes imply. But
I expected more. ☉

Brattleboro

The bridge stretched across the wide
river, silver in overcast afternoon.
I crossed to dripping woods, dense and green,
and walked by water, meaning to ease
my inner turmoil, walking only, not
thinking, except at first about the
wet, the close cool air, the streams
across the path frequent and loud.
I turned back, finally, when two
orange posts appeared. I recrossed
the bridge, stopped dead center to
watch wet bright skin move under me.
I returned to the bench where a
stranger waited, though I'd come to
visit him and had meant to share
his bed that night. I wouldn't. Instead
we'd drive north in the dark, I'd
listen to more of his confusion, but
feel my anger fade, overtaken by
the puzzles we tried to sort through,
even as their pieces morphed before us,

within us. "This is a watershed," I said,
and much more. Did he hear me? Late we drove
around the quiet town, the posh Inn the only
choice. Finally he said, "I'm sorry this is
happening this way." It stuttered out, barely
audible. We walked together down
circular stairs into the misting night.
"I hope this won't be too hard on you,"
I said. "I think it might be," he said, still
a stranger, still a cipher, even to himself. ☉

Along the Gila, April

Stars bright through junipers, river
rush, frogs in noisy love. We sat on
thermarests, pots from dinner turned
over on red space blanket, candle lantern
between us. You told me more of the dull
greyness from your childhood, the response to
your lively color: they tried to
beat you back to grey. And forty years
later, despite your escape, despite your
mind, despite your explorations, despite
your life filled with many people and riches
of emotional release, the grey persisted,
washing over your color: the color had
ceased to bloom. My heart hurt.
But I knew more about your lingering inner
greyness and grasped my difficulty—
to balance what I needed with what
I could do to help you find what might
still blossom among the ashes. ✺

Who to Trust?

Concoct explanations from thin air,
chimeras of inner needs, images
unrelated to him?
She stands accused of that,
and other things, prime among them of
having deeper feelings than he, second
of having more desire. Yet it is not
unrequited, wholly, and he feels pulled to
her for reasons not quite clear.
Perhaps in his accusations he's grateful for
her claimed transgressions; perhaps
more prone to build his own
spectral shades which float
only partly embodied in the ether of
the imaginal. But with words attached,
and bodies, their two human hearts
sometimes hurt, sometimes simply
beat gently. She doesn't know if she
is guilty of the charges, has no judge or
jury to help her sort it out, though she
knows no one can be trusted as much as
she trusts herself. And yet she doesn't
know, beyond not trusting her accuser's
eyes, wanting the evidence explored together
in a court not of law, not of stained
oak, hard benches, and interminable
procedures, but where the river cuts the
canyon, the cottonwoods leaf out, and
words slip away on wind. The wind
feels so young. How else to say it?
The wind feels so young. ☙

Hunger

At least, she thought, he's not simply
reacted to her because she stepped forward,
holding her heart in her hands. Others,
he said, lately had done the same. But
then she understood: he saw mostly
her gesture, the offer, the approach
and felt himself the source of her
movement, the magnet that drew her.
Less he saw her heart, what she offered
him of herself, what she offered him
of himself, through the circling
dances, the interlocking words. She
grasped it finally: the power she
gained simply by seeking him, opening
herself to his whims. But what she'd
opened in him was not what she'd hoped:
a hunger to explore together.
She'd opened a different hunger, an old
hunger, with its matching antidote: the
hunger to be loved above all else, to fill
an emptiness which can't be filled, the hunger
which finally made him feel weak. Its
antidote: to keep distant, to disempower her.
The hunger, its mated weakness and its antidote
had less to do with her than the stars turning
in the night sky. Yet she kept her hands in
front of her, toward him, her heart
resting on their upturned palms. ๑

Closed on Air

Possession. Possess. Hold it in your hands
and believe you can grasp it forever;
but then you realize to hold one thing
enslaves your hand. What you intend
to keep fast, not let get away, holds
your fingers and thumb and palm much more
completely than you could ever hold it.
Your hand, in possessing, is stopped
entirely from moving. Better open the
fingers and believe that is the only way
to hold anything: to keep near, to
keep your own ability to point and
touch and clap and thread a needle.
I know this, I learned it when I first
fell in love, though perhaps I knew it
already, feeling my hand neither gloved nor
bandaged, nor in a tight fist, as
freedom—but a freedom hidden, not
easily visible, so more possible, more
successful. Hold a pen and write. It
is not the pen you care about, not the
pen that matters, its narrow barrel
resting on the fleshy skin between thumb
and forefinger, its clip reflecting silver;
but the words, which the hand can never
hold, never possess. How can anyone think
otherwise? How can love ever lead to such an
illusion, to the gripped immobile fingers,
closed on air?
Empty. ✇

A Small Poke With a Cactus Spine

A small poke with a cactus spine,
an accidental cut with an exacto knife,
hitting my head hard on the top of the garden door,
stepping on a wet log in the forest and
sliding sideways to land with a thud. Not
bad hurts, not past healing, but sudden and
unexpected, partly due to inattention,
partly to some molecular configuration:
bad luck.

You've hit me somehow: slapped
me, or kicked me in the shin, or thrown a
snowball with a rock embedded, grazing
my temple. And yet perhaps you don't even
know your flailing arms have caught me
like a punch.
Or perhaps you're simply engrossed in
your complicated, wild dance and
I happened to come within range, to get
clipped in the side by your swinging arm,
swatted alongside my head with your open hand,
so the world spun for awhile.
Hurt from inattention. Yours.

Would it be better if you'd meant to cause
me pain? How strange, even, for me to
think in such terms, taking on your
childhood, not mine, as the operable
metaphor. When I gouged my hand
along the Gila, I almost fainted, but not
quite. I knew what to do to care for
myself. I'd hoped to keep the moon-shaped
scars on my palm. But for their memory,
they've disappeared
completely. ☙

Put A Stone In Your Mouth

Put a stone in your mouth and keep it
there clinking against your teeth,
causing you to mumble, to be
aware of your mouth always, so you
don't swallow it. Worry it with your
tongue, park it between your lower
molars and your cheek. It makes your
saliva flow, lubricating your palate.
Hold its small roundness under your
tongue, a lump like a pea under the
princess's mattress, move it from side to
side, testing its hardness between your
teeth once in awhile. It doesn't get softer,
it doesn't get smaller, it doesn't change
shape. Could you put more stones
in your mouth so they bump against
each other, adding other tones to
the oral percussive possibilities?

You want so much to bite down on it, hoping
it will crack open to a soft center like a
geode filled with honey, but you know
you can't: your teeth would break first.
But can you spit it out, the smoothed
mineral, so you can eat easily again? No.
No more than you can grow a tail, or put
extra joints in your legs, give yourself
prehensile toes, add six inches to your
height or
leave who you are behind. ⊚

Again and Again

Within repeated dailiness
I watch my own uncertainty as if it were
a lab specimen.

Early sun filters through the growing cane,
shadows indistinct and fragmented across
pale carpet, across legs still in
fuzzy pants against the morning chill.
Low rumble from freeway traffic half a
mile away, bird chirps, a grackle
squawk, distant hammering. Cool air
through open door. I think of turning
the compost, of putting in tomato plants,
of washing the rug, of taping *Justine* and
Mountolive for a friend, of whether I might
borrow his kayak to go down the Yampa.

My specimen uncertainty: I take it out again for
dissection, smell its formaldehyde. Though
I've cut it up before, the wrinkled
organs have miraculously regenerated, so
I can slice away connective tissue with
my sharp scalpel again to see how the
pancreas and spleen and gall bladder rest
near the stomach. I can cut again the
stomach's tough rind to reveal the inner
convolutions, and find again the stones
I inadvertently swallowed, their smooth
sides impervious to living digestive juices,

immune to formaldehyde, hard enough
to break my scalpel's blade. The core of my
uncertainty is revealed again and again,
but never found on any map of its arcane
anatomy. ☉

I'd Murdered You

I'd murdered you, but regretted it.
Besides, what if they found out and
arrested me? You lay immobile in
some room not close, not too far, on
your back, on your bed. I fretted,
I mourned, I grieved, I worried
about the "authorities"—who were they?
No one seemed as distraught as I'd
expected, but they planned your service.
You lay on the ground, wrapped
everywhere except your face.
Arms, legs, torso, but you were contorted like
a creature not quite human. And I
saw you move! As if you needed to
escape your chrysalis. Maybe! Maybe you
weren't dead after all. I went to you,
leaned over. You still moved, stretching
almost, but you weren't conscious, not alive
again. I spoke, "Come back, at least
come back for me. If you love me, come back
to this world," I begged. "Do you love me?"
I asked in a plaintive woman's voice. How
many times has that been asked? Then you
looked at me full for a moment, eyes wide,
and said, "Yes, but not enough." ☙

New York

On the stage two men stood facing
the full audience, no props. In the
plot they stood against a camp fence
in Nazi Germany, imprisoned because
they loved men. They stared out at us
but addressed each other, twenty feet apart.
"I lick your cock." "I run my hand
from your armpit down your side across
your belly between your legs under
your balls." They continued until we all
squirmed in our seats. The power of words:
they live on physical memory, they live by
themselves, they live as they were spoken
by living men, to a living audience, in a
contrived scene. The two men spoke as if we
weren't there, aware we were. They spoke through
layers of history and invented worlds. We heard
with our bodies and our blood flowed faster,
our erectile tissues engorged, our breaths
picked up speed—we were all transgressing some
boundaries, we were all engrossed in the story,
we were all engulfed in our own sexual lives,
our memories and desires, our futures and pasts,
imaginations like caresses, like flesh on
flesh, but in words, in that setting more
memorable than the fuck with your lover
last week, more attuned with your
hair-trigger inner spark than a kiss
on your own warm neck. ☙

Section 7

Ecologies of the Heart: Cycle II

Question the world.
Question yourself. Question not
for answers, but for the attitude
of questioning, for the meandering
response which will take you down roads
unimagined. To question means you don't
know but are curious and will listen.
Question the wind and the water, the
heavens milky with stars; but more
than that, question the faint steam
rising from your tea, question the
owl's wing, question the wood of your
table top, the wool of your sweater,
dark green and smelling of sage smoke.

Ask questions of your lover, but don't expect
your curiosity satisfied, don't expect a
neat package like questions and answers on a
test. This is not a test. This is an owl's
wing, the memories of mountains, and the
stones on the trails to the tops of mountains,
the hawk circling below, the wind, the trails
down. This is not a test: this is the waves
breaking on a black beach, the soft sand
in ridges as you wade out. This is the
phosphorescence at night that follows
your bodies as they glide through
the salty wet. ◉

In cold night the hot pools steamed,
fogging the stars, baking our bodies,
raking the silence with splash and
rush of spring water arcing from
its source into moving flow where
we sat, waist deep, warmed, exploring
the gravel bottom, the rocks, the short
wooden benches someone had made and left
for all unknown soakers. We could see,
but not well; we could hear, but not well.
We sat closer than we had before, our bare
thighs and arms touching lightly. You didn't
move away. I didn't move away. And we
both noticed. I thought, "Trouble? No,
this is safe." Cold drops formed in mid
air, fell in sudden pointed thrills on
foreheads, shoulders. We sat alone among
firs and granite rocks, the canyon steep
below, leaving only star-rich sky, hot
mist; our words stayed light, loose,
our minds innocent, unaware, our bodies
in the primal wash knowing past any
knowing. When we talked about it later,
we agreed on facts: "Here's a bench
for two," I said and you hopped over.
Without thought I melted into you.
The utter basics.
"We probably shouldn't do too much of this,"
I said as we stood in the knee-deep water and
you hoisted me onto your hips, the cold air
no longer cold, the air no longer air,
our bodies pure light. ๑

Mapping

Can he understand the way your hand bends at
its wrist when you're explaining the
reasons scarlet runner beans need
pole teepees, or the way the snake disappeared
between tree roots? What is more erotic
than to try to understand another? To
abandon the pampered focus on yourself
and try to grasp an attitude that grows
from a history as unlike yours as ancient
Rome differs from the Green River flowing
through orange cliffs. Watch the delicate
folds around eyes and understand
the shapes his words define may be
clear, but so strange you seem to see
through wavery water filled with
bubbles. The more details you find,
the more parts begin to work together,
the more you're taken out of yourself, the
more pleasure and release for both.
You see his upper arms, twice as wide
as yours, you see them taper to his narrow
wrists, you see his long fingers, you watch
them move in the air: the river goes around
a bend, his fingers say, and the hot spring
is just at the base of a cliff, back from
the water, across a gravel beach. His fingers
drop again to his thighs, quiet. ◐

To be in two places at once
stretches ligaments and tendons
past anything imagined in dance class,
torso folded over outstretched legs,
hamstrings pulling a little against
their tightness, lower back releasing
vertebrae by vertebrae, the tiny spaces in
sacrum loosening, mouth, finally,
close enough to knees so you can
bite them if you wanted; and legs spread
wide apart on the floor, inner thighs
and those soft tissues at your femurs' heads
all that's holding you back from splits
the twenty-year-olds revel in, their fronts lying
flat before them, their mobile hips open, open,
so legs angle bodies to a leotarded "T."

To be in two places at once
stretches the softest tissues—
the ones where no muscle bundles contract
and relax in an ionic soup—the tissues
which slide across each other in memory,
where warm-up proceeds not by counts
of eight, repeated, but by counts of fifteen
or nine-and-a-half or thirty-one. And once
you're warm enough to dance, you leave
the floor, the class dissolves to space
or into sunrise or dried coneflowers
or a round stone. And you're warm. What
might once have felt like contorting has
stretched to fluid movements, elastic
space and time, reflecting back as if two
places were after all just different parts
of the same glowing whole. ☙

A Good Family Man

One crow calls, the rough
repeated note penetrating adobe
walls. Cold January but bright
sun. The only picture of my uncle Hobart
is from Deming, in a raincoat over bare
legs, in sunglasses—out for the cure, maybe,
no one knows. He was the black sheep, I've
been told, not a good family man, so
the divorce was OK. What does that mean?
He drank, he fucked, he made no money,
he wandered away? I do not know, know
only my father, his younger brother,
felt the weight of right behavior. But
is my DNA inscribed somehow with
my uncle's rangy ways? But—no
use, only speculation. I've gone to childhood
for telling moments; a distant uncle's life
can't help much. The crow has quieted.
A good family man—I've never wanted
one, not wanting to be a good family
woman, and yet I feel the pull now.
Cold outside. But the sun through
the south window will warm the front room
all day. I'll talk to you later. A good
family man, caught in the grip of an
ideal image with fangs. You want out. You've
found in me, in this dry land, an
escape, the cure. Can you take it?
But do I want you, a good family man? ☉

Winter Chaco

Camped in Chaco by a fire
against bitter cold, I read you dreams
dreamed in the Gila. You listened,
attentive, present. As we sat half
hot, half freezing, far away my mother
dreamed she'd lost me—dreamed *her* mother
in vivid presence, standing with an angel.
My mother asked the two if they knew where
to find me, always the wayward child. And
my grandmother, with her ethereal hair,
looked sad beyond bearing, not wanting to
tell, but finally said, "She fell—she's gone."
My mother woke with a start, not knowing
I'd gone to the canyon filled with time
and history and the shades of long-gone beings,
their skeletal stone structures as telling
and as beautiful as bleached bones. I hadn't
fallen, I hadn't gone farther than down the
road. Gone, I wonder, who else might
be gone? What else? I read you more than the
dreaming tale, I read you about my life as
woman, my resistance to an enforced shape;
but also about my hard-won match of my mother's
struggles against expectations, about her own
mother's refusal to be held down, held back,
held to a static show.
The words lifted with cedar sparks,
faded into icy night, bounced off
rocks, gone with the fire's light. ✆

Robe of Raw Silk

You are a robe of raw silk,
rough, not slinky, sheen among
coarse strands, color of oatmeal
or freshly cut pine branches,
outer bark stripped. I feel my
shoulders rub against your silk—
smooth and rough at once. You are
ripe vegetables just picked,
warm skin of summer squash, eggplant,
tomatoes, ungainly fava beans
in their pods, red sweet peppers
hiding many seeds in convoluted
inner reaches. I taste you, meal by meal.
You are sitar music, with its rhythms
unlike rhythms from childhood, slides and
bends disrupting well-tempered scales—
but you live uneasily in such
rhythms, in such variable pitches,
hoping always to make yourself a
motet, harmonics vibrating into
open sky. Your plucked strings
pull me beyond a regular beat, past
a scale with only white keys and
black keys, into chanting, birdsong,
whale music; your pulse pulls me into
rhythms and counter rhythms from the
ocean floor, water shaken into waves by
lava erupting into dark wet depths. ☙

The Gate

At some distance attempts to
make sense start, woven with memory
and desire; does the sense I make
embrace worry more than possibility?
Do I see barbed wire more than long summer
grasses on the fence's other side? On
this side? For whatever has changed
has not shattered the world, but
only opened a gate, wide and creaking
between two pastures not grazed for
years so the ground hasn't been
trampled, the plants not nibbled to
nubs, but grown tall enough to bloom,
seed heads hanging heavy, beating
in time to the wind and the pull
of their weight, anchored to the ground.
The gate: weathered wood, no barbed
wire. I see now—the fences only give sign
men have been here, ordering the land,
making provisional divisions,
temporary lines over the rises, but their
fences are permeable, and never
permanent, despite their tenacity.
The gate's no longer latched and even the
illusion of separation means less and
less. The gate never stopped the wind,
never kept seeds from sprouting
in the next field, always stood as a
sign only, a barrier only in name.
And we've crossed it.
In both directions
we've crossed it. ✆

Sheets I

I've bleached the sheets in the tub
and one hangs whitely out the
door in front of me, blown by wind,
still damp, leaf shadows moving across it.
No blood, no stains, just a dingy greyness
from many nights alone; no crusty love spots,
no memories. White canvas, white paper,
white sheets; cotton, cool, bright. Stark white.
Not antiseptic; open and simple. Elegant and
basic. But white: Moby Dick meditations,
cold, ominous. The Sikhs wear white, or
is it the Sufis? Snow, weasels in winter
called ermines, ice, crescent ends of my
fingernails, my eyes, minus their irises and
blood vessels, this house's inner walls.
Swan feathers by the bed, arranged in the blueberry
pot, smooth glaze mottled maroon—long
white feathers joined with a macaw's blue.
White. Bleached. Cotton, catching
wind. Clouds, fog. Bones. Ivory. White
stones. Wool. I resist purity, milk, white bread.
The white—this bleached sheet lifting and
falling out my door calls to me
"hot skin on coolness, summer dawns
entwined with bodies, the boat
which takes you to deep forgetfulness,
sails into deep remembering." ✆

Sheets II

The wind woke me in the night,
moving trees in rushing rackets.
I turned out of covers, hot;
I snuggled back under, cold, cool
air blowing through open door; I
woke and curved my arm around the
softest pillow, filled with down, slid
my legs to a cool quadrant of the cotton
sheets; I slept and dreamed an old lover
and his mate passed me leaving the
concert: he apologetic, she gloating, again and
again. The wind disappeared, I slept;
the wind returned, I woke. The moon
brightened the room, a silver patch on
louvered closet doors. I turned over,
I turned back, the sheets molded over
my body, gentle weight, caressing. I thought, half
awake, of how it's been sleeping alone,
of how it is sleeping again next to another,
reaching out in sleep to grasp a hand, an
arm encircling me from the back, kissing a
palm, feeling my shoulder brushed with a cheek.
I sleep little, awake at every flop next to
me, but it's not like being wakened by the
wind racing outside at a distance.
The body next to me has no armor; we're
enclosed together in smooth cotton.
Pressed against you I sleep dreamless.
I wake to feel your weight of
dreaming ease beside me. ✆

Wind / Not Wind

Moving away from, moving toward.
Do we feel those forces as the same,
and if not the same, then complements of each
other, as the wind blowing past: moving away
from, moving toward, no fixed
destination, no fixed point of origin —
the only point where we stand, how
we see from our temporary rooted
spot. The metaphor of wind. But
metaphors can cloud the issues,
obscure the situation, fuzz the heart,
fuzz our understanding of others'
hearts. You have a place, a moving place,
a life to move away from, a universe
to move toward. You are not wind, but
the forces still rise from both
directions. And they defy
a simple view. Your destination
pushes you away, a dragging anchor
pulls you back.

Love this land and it will love
you in return. There's help here.
But *there* others depend on
you and resent it. You hate their
dependence, you hate their resentment
and are hurt by it. Yet their lives mirror
your own: they want away, they want to move
outward; they are held by invisible webs as you
are held, frozen by fear. But
we all must keep moving. We have only
the choice of how we fling
our bodies into the racing air.
We don't have the choice to stop. ☙

Flood

Opaque, you said, my life looks opaque to
me. I can't see my way clear. I don't know
what's next. I need a new mission statement.

You lay among cotton sheets
disordered like stream banks three weeks
after a flood, plants ripped out,
torn limbs and leaves in messy piles, but
new shoots poking up, drenched with fecund
flood water, reviving, pruned, not wounded.

Lying on your back, you looked at the ceiling,
answering my questions with sentences minus
their last words.

On either side, you said, I have a woman: one
dressed in leather with a whip howling how she feels,
telling me what to do. It enrages me. The other is
concerned about what is Right, the Correct Image.
She works on me with needles.
I answer her by going to sleep.

I said, again, you're right, they hold you on
either side, but don't you want to move forward
neither in rage, nor asleep?

I lifted my bare leg over yours, the early sun
glowed on white sheets, white walls.
Neither woman flanking you was me.
Inside: my own flood, my own new green shoots. ❧

The Wing

On the table by the bed the blueberry
pot filled: white swan wing feathers
molted by the pond behind Moonstone Beach,
one hyacinth macaw's from Sally's
tail at the Providence zoo, a redtail's tail feather
from a friend who has a federal permit,
one from a roadrunner, a little chewed, and a
handful of black ones: from crows or ravens.
Walking by the ditch on Christmas Day I found
a pair of crow wings, the remaining meat of their
shoulder joints still bloody where the coyote
had ripped them from three bites of body,
two graceful soft sculptures, dark
against the dry path. I gave you the left one,
the one more spread, though not
fanned entirely open. For your left
sandal, as Hermes, grin raising your beard. By
the blueberry pot filled with feathers the
white sheets lie in disorder, though I've
slept in them alone for five days, your
body gone—your body with its well-behaved chest
hair lying so smoothly between your
dark nipples. I remember the first time
I touched their ordered patterns in a kind of
rapture—your body is in snowy New England,
your black wing stored in my back closet.
Take the wing in your mind, in your
heart, and use it: no one will expect
you to rise into the clouds, into the
cold blowing snow. Surprise can be everything.
Fly. ⚭

The Mountain

Does distance make things clear?
In this light unimpeded by trees,
the mountain sixty miles off takes on
a presence, a shape hard to track
from ten miles. Two miles.
Touch distance. Your sister warns,
"Go slow." We don't disagree. Your
sister warns, with less quotable
language, "You meant to find your
own center. Doesn't love interfere
with that?" We see the danger.
But love has helped me always
to grow into myself, watered deeply,
fertilized, photosynthesis on overdrive.
I don't know what her warning means to
you, surrounded now by snowless hills,
converted farmhouses, generations of
silent men, their women wanting and made
shrewish by deep hungers. I breathe
this cold bright air, watch the sun
climb adobe walls, see the mountain
in the distance, know my own center
belongs here, and on the mountainside,

but know my view of you is *obscured* by
distance, my inner mirages floating
peacefully. Jung says you can be in the
valley, fighting in the war, or watch it
from the mountainside: it looks quite
different. Is it the same war? The mountain
can be climbed, its trails winding
invisible from here. But I have climbed
them, and have felt their turns and
inclines, boulders and rubble. The
mountain. Is the mountain the
same mountain? ✆

Back There

I

What must it take for you to imagine
killing yourself? Or if you're only
saying that, what must it mean
about your sense of powerlessness?
About the extremes you feel you must go
to get the kind of attention you need?
I've known you nearly thirty years
and I've never seen your despair. Can
it ever be quieted? I know I am not
the cause, but the man you show your
need loves me, and I am
implicated. I feel him pull away from me,
drawn back to your needs; and my heart,
filled with compassion for you, for your
free-floating pain, turns in my breast.
I am stricken, surprised to be woken in
the night by my own tears. I have always
thought, my mind alert to conditions,
histories, personalities, "He's too caught,
he won't leave. He will shrivel back there,
but the cords are strong." With a certain
dispassion. Clear-eyed, not happy, but
grounded. I hoped, regardless. But now I
feel it, feel the loss of possibility, for
him, for me, and I ache. Your ache is old,
I know, it merely changes form. I don't discount
it, I don't understand it. But I see it growing,
recruiting other pain in an effort to
cure itself, a futile kind of effort.

I have no answer.

No. I will not be so passive. I have no
answer except to speak, to feel this pain,
sudden and surprising,
to speak of it in its particulars,
to feel its sharp edge. ☙

II

His message startled me, flickering
up on the screen at dinnertime, from
his cold New England landlocked
hills. I feared he'd been swallowed
again: walls built of things,
piles of papers, known conversation,
expected movement, expected silence.
He had begun the slide, but pulled
out. I didn't think he'd do it,
speak his heart when he knew
a tornado would follow. Well. The winds
were already at gale force, the
landscape not bucolic. He spoke
into a storm, a blinding blizzard,
or more accurately, into a
fog which drifted through
bare trees, shapes appearing and
disappearing. A fog at sea, where
water laps the hull and
sudden buoys clang their bells.
Through the fog he spoke.
Did he remember this desert light? ❧

Care

When does caring cross the line
and turn into oppression, the cared-for one
feeling her own strength and competence
sapped? How hard to fight another's
impulse for the good. How hard to
take gestures of love and reject
them because they come with a price.
The cost is loss of self—not
entirely, but small chinks break off;
capacity, not used, atrophies. Can the
lover not see that? Or is he blinded by
his own need to give? Is such need met
by love in return, or does that matter?
"I care for you, enfold me in thanks." It seems
too pat. But is it another version of those
little boys who wanted to help me hammer
when I could hammer better even if
I was a girl? They assumed I couldn't, took no
time to see and wanted to do it themselves
to show their hammering skill. I never
let them, always incensed at their blindness,
incensed they treated me like an inferior. A
girl. Is that it? Partly. And yet.
Real need exists. And me—the other side—
where does competence cross the line and
become a barrier? And can I simply turn the
tables, caring for another to feel my own
strength? Ah. There it is. Caring for another
must be for the other to feel her strength, not
weakness, and requires
a different kind of love. ◈

Gallup

For now you live in the quintessential Western
town a century after Romance: red rock
cliffs, rodeo grounds, Navajos in pickups,
fast food by the interstate, the old hotel
with pix of movie stars housed and fed
for cowboy flicks, Hollywood in the desert: fake
stories, real sky, real space.
Your temporary digs have views of busy tracks,
trains calling like hungry animals all night,
of the freeway filled with trucks, of the mesa
north of town winter dry, of old Route 66
alive with old pawn in vaults; your three
rooms furnished with fake flowers, a white couch and
matching chair, a high-end stereo with speakers
large enough to hide coyotes. You're still hiding
from your life, sorting out the changes:
temporary from permanent. I drive two
hours, blessed again and always by the light,
craving time with you. You spend long hours seeing
Indians with the flu; meet a shaman who
helps drug-addicted kids but needs
aspirin for his fever. I sleep off my own
viral pall while you talk to your
Eastern life: you're hiding but not
off the grid. The words hang like dusty
damask inside the house, in your mind.

Outside, the desert night opens to lights
blinking from a hundred miles, another
freight bellowing past. I wake, we cook
broccoli and steak, potatoes and mushrooms,
I speak from high mesas, land without
swamps or mildew; I call to you.
You want to hear, you know what you've left, but
don't yet know how you fit this new land,
if you fit this new light, where to find
the pattern you can weave yourself into,
where to find yourself. ✆

Shaman

You'd been visiting a Navajo in
his suburban ranch house; he claimed
to be a shaman, saw images in coals
next to a carved white buffalo,
a stone horny toad, said your intuition
was blocked by anger, by hiding behind
your doctor's mask, by withholding
information from your wife.
You'd been pulled in, taken with his insight,
no matter how obvious his rap. After midnight
when you touched my bare shoulder
I rose from deep sleep to your single sentence,
"I'm supposed to sleep alone tonight
to consolidate the healing." Ears unfiltered by
my waking self, I heard hatred of women,
of the body; I heard your credulity,
blindness; I heard your retreat
from contact; I felt myself brushed
aside for a wooden nickel, a sneering
slap at Eros. And from my depths rose a
fury I couldn't contain, didn't want to
contain. The distance of your body, your
silence read like control, braille I couldn't
ignore. I knew it in my blood: I didn't want
to control you, but I would not be
strapped down, put in my place, accused
without words of interfering with your
wholeness. You tried at first to stop me,

then simply watched as I packed the
truck, thawed frozen ropes on the back
with my bare hands, drove away east.
I sobbed into the night; in an hour
I turned back. For myself. I knew I ran
from my own burning coal. Three days later
I still wonder if my fury will
always be called up by something in you. ☙

On Navajo Land

We stood under towers named Church Rock
in cold sun. Above us, across
bare sandstone, peach and cream,
skittered many sheep—or were they goats?—
strung out, followed by two then
three rez dogs, then three puppies, dark
spots on the bleached landscape, all running
so far away they ran silently. Then the
herder crossed, in a faded pink shirt hot
in wind-shaped rock, a sweatshirt
hood against the cold. She—or he?—disappeared
behind the far rise, then reappeared, looking
back at us, unmoving, alert, a speck of humanness:
our momentary look into days
repeated and repeated. Next to me Sylvia
waved and the herder turned away,
slipped below curved pale stone,
followed sheep and dogs. We hiked on up,
four Anglos, all past fifty, all herding
our own sheep, sometimes following them
across high trails, sometimes leading them;
the grass sparse and dry, the world overlapping
our travels here and there: selling our wool,
making our rugs, turning away as strangers wave.

But mostly we cross the rocks and hills alone
with the dogs and sheep, taking in the rough
land, stark and vast, never knowing what's beyond
that next rocky ridge. ❀

Rock Creek Pottery

We sat on their deck, weathered grey,
lichen sprouting even from the solid chairs; we
ate olives and almonds, rice cakes and green
tea. Moist spring, leafy engulfment. In their
house: many rough stoneware platters from
Japan, legions of their own pots, dark log walls,
dark wood floor, skylights open to the
mists. I'd brought you to these old friends: a
college roommate who'd found her match
twenty years back. In their barn: a simple
showroom, bowls and vases and teapots arranged
on shelves. In their pottery: kickwheels, a
light patina of dried clay everywhere. In
their bathroom: a dark blue sunken tub, an
original Hokusai print. In their guestroom:
a PowerMac and new HP printer. In the
morning we found a spotted orange salamander
in the blooming vinca—I'd never seen one;
as a kid, you'd found them by the hundreds.
That evening you told them about
your topsy-turvy life, they told us
about diving among spawning groupers in
the Caribbean, I told them about mountain
lions in the Gila, they told us about
becoming Zen monks, then Zen masters, then
stopping zazen altogether because ego had
intruded like a dragon. The next morning
we drove down the mountain, through blinding rain
on the interstate, finally to the ocean, where
lightning flashed silently for hours. ◈

Present

Now they all say. That's the
answer, the only answer. And I
gaze out at the garden in the half
light of a snowy dawn, yellow
grasses nearly white; I feel the
tea's warmth in my mouth, washing
down my throat; note my left hand's
cool fingers on my cheek, my chin resting
in its palm. Present. Now. But to
be human is to remember other quiet
times, to feel them in my cells, to remember
other snows, even other snows in this garden,
so hungry for moistness. To be human
is to know in two hours I will choose
white potatoes, sweet potatoes, celery from the
bins of winter vegetables, will take the
medium hot chile out of the freezer for the
green chile stew I will make in case
you're hungry for food when your drive
across snowy desert ends at my door,

when you'll step into my warmth, smelling
of cold air, smiling, when I'll put my
body inside your arms, when I'll put
my arms around your warm being, when
I'll pay attention to any differences
you grew into while you sat, breathing
for ten days silently, but among others,
when I'll pay attention to any changes in
myself, remembering how I was a month ago
when you left.
Now it will be in ten hours.
Ten hours from now. ◐

Inner Weather

Fronts move through
with storms washed in blood, calms
of sleep, or the strange cloud formations
which appear and disappear in dreams
over rainforests, sun sliding below
green to illuminate everything at
sunset. Winds blow in from due west,
carrying dust fogs, particles from
the past which cling together like
solid objects and are gone as quickly as
they came. Flash through. Like anger
in children. Or the predictability
of summer afternoons: conditions are
right, the ground of being has sucked up
heat, emotional ferment has begun to
steam and bake, spilling itself into the
air, provoking thunderheads like
mountains, and the rains come, short
and drenching, releasing the feeling, not
as anger, not the outburst of a cloudburst
but as a wave of insight, a gush of words,
quickly building, quickly releasing. A
fast turn around, the loneliness gone, the
hunger passed. Or filled. Sometimes
drought lingers; but sometimes wet weather
fills the rivers 'til they overflow their banks,
flooding the bosque, flooding the trees in my
grove whose branches twist in contorted
grace, whose roots, flood or not, always drink
from deeper sources than I can ever see. ☺

Love What You Love

Flash flood warnings. Thunder at dawn.
Rain on skylight so loud it overpowered
dreams, thoughts, worries, plans. I burrowed
under covers, listening to the oddity
of weather, beating waves from the sky.
I got up once and opened the
back door to smell it—not cold, just
wet, like being inside dessert,
lemon mousse or chilled fruit. I crawled
back to dry warmth, glad I slept in
my house, not in down under a nylon
tarp in a canyon where the way out
required a ford across a crotch-high
river, fast and brown. I rearranged my
legs to move my hip, sore from yesterday's
run—no not the run, but my age, my years
dancing, that old injury, the long ago
mugging. Love what you love as well as you
can, I learned in the canyon last week. Yes.
But more: make what you make with love and
make it all well enough so the love is
powerful, so it lives unextinguished
outside in the world, alive enough
to be felt. Felt when you're not there.
Alive enough to trigger flash flood
warnings, thunder at dawn,
lightning flashes along another's spine. ☙

Section 8

Coda

Along the Rio Chama, Toward Winter Solstice, 1999 (a sestina*)

What geometric order wouldn't the celadon waves abandon to fashion
        their translucent turbulence,
The stream's coiling and uncoiling patterns bordered now by icy lapidary spirals?
In summer the space above whispers words so insubstantial the violet-green swallow
Swoops through them as if she knew her bones
Weighed no more than air itself. In the eye of the raven
The jade river reflects back winter sun, wavering between banks thick with sage.

What backwash across the sand flats has nourished the sage,
Tonguing the little bluestem and stipa with a necessary turbulence
Until *Artemisia's* moon-green leaves, like tiny hands, three fingers stretched skyward,
        grew with their raven
Stems in endless ranks? Slower than the widening spiral
Of a snail shell, they spread outward to cover bones
From hazy pasts, bones the sand itself would not swallow.

What molecular recall restores the angling speed of the swallow
After she sips from the current's skin and lifts herself back into empty air? What sage
Advice might she give us if we could only hear with our bones?
Behind her sickled wings, invisible to all but suspended cottonwood dust,
        brief turbulence
Opens the channels between earth and sky, offering in their fugitive spiral
Forms hints of how we might understand, if we could only laugh like the distant raven.

What incendiary secrets smolder like underground coal fires in the raven
Night, where owl wings flash darkness across the stars and I swallow
An ancient unease that has curled along my spine like a whelk's expanding spiral?
In a silence promising solace as primal as the fragrant smoke from burning sage,
The night counterbalances the skin-smooth known with a combustible
        unknown turbulence,
And hot fleeting flames ripe with imagined answers singe my bones.

What trick of color allocation has aligned patched snow with sun-bleached bones?
Cold collects in the shadows along flaxen hillsides and under flame-shaped junipers
        where yesterday a raven
Rested before continuing his survey of the river's watershed. The turbulence
Of summer rains flooding from mesa tops carves the land as surely as the swallow
Carves the air, but with more enduring sign. Along one cliff, sage-
Colored soil erodes; in summer memory a dust devil streaks across the flats
        in a superheated spiral.

What cycling tension propels our inner helical fires, the molecular spiral
Spring we share with down-drifting detritus of ancient seas, the bones
Of these hills now thinly covered in dry skins of grass and sage?
No answer. But this: You have followed the contours of this land as carefully as the raven
Maps a cliff edge. You have dabbed the river's mud, word by word,
        as persistently as the swallow
Has made her rock-protected nest. You have ridden the invisible turbulence.

Between my fingers I smell the sage; in memory I see one wild grape tendril spiral
Around the latch to the open gate. The river's foaming turbulence vibrates in my bones
And I guess the finest trick of the raven. In the cold air I dream I loop upward
        faster than any flashing swallow. ◎

—19 December 1999

---

*"The sestina is like a thin sheet of flame, folding and infolding upon itself."

            —Ezra Pound